The Kogan Page Market Research Series breaks new ground in market research publishing. While most books tend to be all-embracing tomes covering every aspect of market research, each title in this new series is devoted to a specific technique or key area.

The prime aim of the titles in the series is to demystify the technicalities of market research by providing concise, digestible introductions, presented in a clear and comprehensive style.

Well-illustrated throughout, these practical guides will serve as vital introductions for those new to market research, useful revision tools for students and essential refreshers for all market research professionals.

Titles in the series are:

Questionnaire Design
Interviewing
Sampling and Statistics

Future titles will cover:

Desk research
Reporting and presenting data
Analysis and modelling

02. FEB.

ABOUT THE AUTHOR

■

Paul Hague is a Chairman of Business and Market Research PLC. He regularly contributes to the market research trade press and lectures at seminars on the subject. He is author of *The Industrial Market Research Handbook* and co-author of *Do Your Own Market Research, How to do Marketing Research* and *Market Research in Practice*. He is also joint editor of *A Handbook of Market Research Techniques*. All these books are published by Kogan Page.

INTERVIEWING

Paul Hague

KOGAN
PAGE

First published in 1993

Kogan Page Limited
120 Pentonville Road
London N1 9JN

© Paul Hague, 1993

British Library Cataloguing in Publication Data
A CIP record for this book is available from the British Library.
ISBN 0 7494 0918 5

Typeset by BookEns Limited, Baldock, Herts.
Printed in England by Clays Ltd, St Ives plc

CONTENTS

■

PREFACE

∎

The trouble with market research is that so much of it is common sense. I say that it is a problem because the common sense element brings the subject into everyone's domain. For sure, common sense is there at every turn in the process of market research, but that doesn't mean to say that it is an easy subject! Finding out what is going on in the market place and why people act in the way that they do is not so simple that we need only to pop out and ask a few questions.

At times it seems as if many people think of market research as a pastime or a hobby. Young and inexperienced people are asked to 'knock up a questionnaire' in a couple of hours. Students, resting actors and part-timers stand alongside those who have been interviewing for years in many a field-force.

Don't misunderstand me. Market research needs young people — it is very much a young person's job. The work is demanding but interesting and it needs the energies of the young to drive eight hours to achieve just one important interview or to stand in a wind-swept precinct and achieve a quota of thirty interviews in a day. However, market research is not a fill-in activity, it is a serious business providing information to reduce business risk. Interviewing is at the core of market research and, such is its importance, honing these skills is worthwhile for everyone.

Important as it is, interviewing is just one of the tools in the market researcher's tool box. In this book, interviewing takes centre stage. It examines the points of view of the consumer interviewer as well as the business-to-business researcher. It looks at different types of interviews from those which are highly structured and which take place on the telephone or in the street through to the unstructured, probing, depth interview.

Interviewing is part of a much wider process of finding out, including questionnaire design, sampling, report writing and presentation. These equally important subjects are raised in the text and the reader should turn to one of the other books in the series for greater insights into them.

Finally, I would like to acknowledge the help of the many people who have made this book possible. In particular, my long time business partner, Peter Jackson, whose advice and experience over the years have been a considerable influence on me. I have also been shameless in drawing upon chunks of text written by Peter and myself in our other books on market research as I found it difficult to improve on what has already been said.

My friends and colleagues at work have also contributed to the book, probably more than they realise, feeding ideas, being supportive and, above all, providing examples of how true professionals do 'it'.

And last but not least, I must thank the many hundreds of clients at whose expense I have learned my craft over the years. They have had the confidence to commission me and, in the main, they have had the good grace to live with my recommendations. Thanks to them all.

Paul Hague
March 1993

1

INTRODUCTION

■

THE TWO MOST IMPORTANT THINGS IN MARKET RESEARCH

A lecturer I know started selling clothes on a party plan basis to supplement his income and to satisfy an entrepreneurial whim. Soon he was earning twice his salary as a lecturer. The man had long been looking for a way out of academia and eagerly gave up the lecturing post to concentrate on the party plan clothes boom. Within weeks his sales plateaued and very soon they plummeted. The parties which had fuelled the early success in the business had been held by friends and relations whose wardrobes were now bulging with all they wanted or could afford. It proved more difficult than was originally envisaged to find new people to hold the parties and in a very short time the chastened entrepreneur returned to academic life.

On a much larger scale a manufacturer of telecommunications equipment showed handsome profits from its core business of supplying British Telecom with large switchgear. The company was part of a group at whose centre it was considered a star. However, following the heavy investment in new equipment during the 1980s, British Telecom began to reduce its purchases while at the same time technological changes were introducing alternatives to switchgear. For a long time the business's brilliant profit record had masked its disastrous course of a limited customer base and product range.

These two real life examples illustrate how businesses can fail if they do not find out what customers want. In the case of the lecturer's party plan, he was close to his customers but had neglected to look ahead and find out to whom he could sell clothes in the longer term. Similarly, the supplier of switchgear failed to ask enough questions of British Telecom and found itself a hostage to one customer.

Market research is the means by which suppliers of a product or service can find out what their customers want. It is something which astute business people do naturally and often without attaching the label of *market research* to the process. For this reason, market research is often said to be common sense.

Finding out the needs of the customers is at the heart of marketing. Whether this involves asking customers what they want, looking at statistics which show what they are buying or simply observing what is happening on the high street or in industry does not much matter. All have their place in finding out what is going on.

Desk research and observation have their parts to play in identifying the needs of customers but the most common method of all is to talk to people. This brings us to the crux of market research — asking the right question of the right person.

The theme of this book addresses how to find out what is going on by talking to people. However, before this subject is considered in detail, it is worth examining the second part of the axiom, getting hold of the right person.

In a very simple buying situation, such as where a woman goes into a shop to buy a new dress, she is self-evidently in possession of all the information that the market researcher may want to question. How much money does she want to spend? Does she have something specific in mind before going into the shop? Which brands is she aware of? What does she need the dress for? And so on.

Still considering the same woman, let's follow her into a supermarket and watch her buy cereals, razor blades, soap and biscuits — a shopping basket which is not out of the ordinary for most people. We could interview the woman and find out some of the information which led to the purchases, but could she give us the whole truth? Perhaps we would find that her children put in an order for a certain type of cereal, motivated by the promise of a free gift in the pack seen advertised on television. The razor blades were for her husband — she knows he likes a certain brand, though if questioned in any depth maybe she could not say why. The biscuits are family favourites which she has always bought, out of habit as much as anything.

Already we can see that there are some secondary influences creeping into the buying decisions in this supermarket shopping excursion, and the situation is more complicated than was the case when the dress was bought for her own consumption. If the researcher is examining the market for razor blades he has to make decisions as to whether the right person to interview is the person who bought them or the person who uses them or both. Likewise with the cereals and the biscuits.

Take a quantum leap now into an industrial buying situation and think about the people involved in the buying decision for gas separation plants. These are £10 to £20 million investments which sit alongside steelworks or chemical plants and supply the necessary gases required for the production process. The negotiations which lead eventually to the sale of one of these plants takes between one and two years. There would be no less than half a dozen people at the customer's end evaluating the deal with similar numbers on the selling side. The buying team is likely to involve engineers as well as technical experts, production personnel, buyers and general managers. Who should be interviewed? Which questions are appropriate for which people? In protracted negotiations, will people be able subsequently to remember what happened or will events have been fogged by the complexity of the discussions and the passage of time?

It is clear therefore that before we can ask the right questions we need to know something of the buying process so that we can decide at whom the questions should be directed. Deciding who that person should be is just as difficult as formulating the right questions.

WHERE THINGS START TO GO WRONG

THREE TYPES OF COMMUNICATION

Children begin to talk at around the age of two. One of the first uses we make of language is to ask questions. Can I have? Will you give me? Why? Questioning (later we shall call it interviewing) is ingrained in our communications and we take it for granted. Because we have always asked questions and continue to do so in our daily lives, it seems reasonable to assume that it is not too difficult to drum up a few questions for a market research survey. If only it was so simple! Listen in on people talking and their communications can be classified into one of three types:

1. *Conversation*: where people engage in dialogue, sometimes purposeful, sometimes vapid or empty. Conversation is a term which implies that the process is pleasant, involving people who are familiar with each other or there being a lack of formality about the exchange.
2. *Discussion:* a more earnest interchange of ideas, perhaps involving both people equally, maybe centred around a detailed consideration of an idea.
3. *Interrogation:* the intensity of the communication is now at its highest, implying an examination of issues by serious questioning. We have now moved way beyond the pleasantness of conversation to something which implies a certain amount of angst.

After a short contemplation of this classification of the way in which people communicate we can see that interviewing leans more towards interrogation than it does to conversation. Interrogation has someone in control of the interviewing — the interrogator or interviewer! It is hardly surprising, therefore, that the interview, if handled badly, can seem like the 'third degree'. In Utopia, market researchers are likely to hold lots of conversations with people and, in a pleasant and informal way, find out what is going on. However, it is not a perfect world and conversations are too loose a process for uncovering the truth, at least

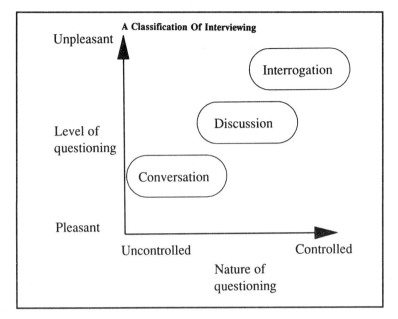

Figure 1.1 A classification of interviewing

on any scale. Think about how people converse. There is banter, people half listen to one another, people talk *at* each other. Clarity, impartiality and rationality are often lacking in ordinary conversation, though they are vital in interviews.

THE IMPORTANCE OF CLARITY

Consider especially the misunderstandings which take place in everyday conversation as people half listen to what is being said or are unclear about whatever they are trying to express. As an exercise, tape and transcribe a conversation and observe how convoluted it is. Sentences finish in half gasp, diction is unintelligible and words are too softly spoken. The choice of words can be confusing, wrong or without meaning to the listener. Everyday conversation is a tortuous exercise which works, by and large, by constant checks and corrections as it progresses.

THE IMPORTANCE OF IMPARTIALITY

Conversation, and especially discussion, is not without its arguments. The advancement of ideas may be biased, but without the prejudice being disclosed, as the perpetrator seeks to win points. The aim of discussion and conversation is enjoyment or the promotion of an idea, whereas the aim of an interview is to discover the truth about what is going on.

THE IMPORTANCE OF RATIONALITY

Logic or reasonableness may not exist in ordinary conversation. What people don't know they may well invent to foster their argument. Unreasonable statements may be made without challenge. This should not happen in the market research interview. Questions need to be logical and reasonable, otherwise people will refuse to answer them, or the silly questions will beget silly answers.

If only we could, we would prefer interviews to be more like conversations or discussions than interrogations. However, we have seen that conversations and discussions lack clarity, and are full of bias and unreasonableness. We may be experts in the art of conversation but this does not make us experts in interviewing or formulating the questionnaires which drive the interviews.

THE ART OF FINDING OUT

Curiosity may have killed the cat but it is a virtue in the character of every market researcher. Some people are too full of their own sense of importance to be interested in others and others are just too polite (or docile) to probe, parry and find out. The market researcher must be none of these things. Possessed with an inquisitive mind the researcher must devise means of wheedling out the information needed.

Imagine that you are alone at a social event and, wishing to meet someone, you decide to engage in conversation. Questions are a wonderful means of introduction and getting to know people, but the choice of question is critical. It would not be a good opening line to ask a person their age or how much they earn; far better to make contact on neutral ground such as their connection with the host, or to use the hackneyed line 'do you come here often?'. The process of questioning and getting to know each other could then follow different avenues, exploring mutual friends, finding out where they live and eventually, only when confidence has been established with the new acquaintance, getting involved in more personal details. During the conversation you will no doubt be subjected to similar questions from the other party and your own self-disclosure will stimulate and encourage a more open exchange.

In this example, questions are the medium by which we get to know someone. Through questioning we find out who people are, make judgements about what they are like, and find out where they are coming from. This process of discovery involves questioning, listening, remembering, offering information and further probing and questioning.

The chat shows on the radio and television are a couple of notches up from the one-to-one informal 'getting-to-know-you' questioning which we engage in on social occasions. The skilled host relaxes guests, gently easing them in with simple questions and only later becoming more pointed. The impression may be that of a fireside chat but it is tightly controlled by the interviewer who has worked out in advance exactly in what direction to take the discussion. In these interviews time is on the host's side and there is an opportunity to 'open up' the guest, allowing for diversions to examine anecdotal footnotes before returning to the principal direction.

Now let us consider the radio or television journalist with just five minutes to uncover the truth from a politician. Here there is little time for the niceties of building a rapport and conversational questioning is out of the window. The journalist has a specific objective, to seek as full an answer as possible in as short a time as possible. Like the chat show host, the journalist has thought through the questions to ask in advance and worked out how certain answers could branch out into different lines of questions — but here there is no time for asides and diversions.

All these different styles of questioning, ranging from the

conversational to the confrontational, can be found in a market research interview. The in-depth interview carried out by an expert qualitative researcher will appear very conversational. However, the researcher will be very much in control, guided by an *aide-mémoire* which ensures that the interview has direction and that all the relevant points are being covered.

In contrast to the depth interview, the street interview gives little time to create an accord and the questions get down to business quickly, rattling along in a highly structured manner. A question is read out, the answer is written down. In this latter case the interviewer who designs the questionnaire is unlikely to be able to achieve a conversation-like informality, but the questionnaire should at least aim to make the interview as pleasurable as possible by adopting a logical sequence to the questions.

AVOIDING TECHNIQUE DRIVEN SURVEYS

Market researchers often have an affinity with one method of data collection and, irrespective of the problem, find their preferred technique can provide the answer. Qualitative researchers favour group discussions or in-depth interviews; quantitative researchers look for hundreds of interviews for an answer; the database 'junkie' may believe that all the answers are already published in some form or another and recommend searching for them by means of electronic desk research.

This is not the way market researchers should work. They should be prepared to open their toolbox and select an *appropriate* tool for the job. The researcher needs a brief from the 'client' (whoever it is that requires the information) and in this brief, hopefully, lies the reason for carrying out the research and what the information will be used for. It is up to the researcher to suggest the most appropriate methods of collecting data, bearing in mind constraints such as the detail of the information required, the timing and any budget limitations.

Whether the interview is apparently informal or obviously highly structured, it should be thought through in advance with either a check-list of questions (for the unstructured interview) or a more structured questionnaire for the larger number of telephone interviews. Mapping out the objectives and designing the questions before the interviews take place ensure that the expensive process of interviewing actually does deliver the information required.

2

OBSERVATION

■

OBSERVATION — ONE OF THE EARLIEST METHODS OF PERSONAL DATA COLLECTION

In early market research, data was collected not by questioning but by observation. Indeed, it was considered that the best way of finding out what people thought was to watch their movements and habits. In the late 1940s and 1950s, teams of observers made notes on all aspects of the daily lives of British people and Mass Observation, one of the UK's oldest market research companies, still carries the legacy of this early methodology in its name.

Today, observation is used wherever it is possible to collect data without actually speaking to the respondent, or where to do so may produce a wrong or ambiguous answer. It plays an important role in researching children, whose powers of expression may not allow them to articulate exactly what they think. Watching children play can be far more revealing. Observation is used in shopping surveys, especially in-store, when the customer is looking at the shelves and deciding what to buy. It is used to discover how things are done in practice, for instance, the way that people open packs of biscuits and how they read instructions can sometimes be more honestly answered by observation than by questioning.

Observation also has a role to play in industrial market research. It can be used to assess the size of a plant, see how a tool is used, or identify what products are bought. Observation does not necessarily involve face-to-face contact with a respondent or customer but it almost always requires the presence of the interviewer. On the grounds that it is a personal research method, it qualifies for inclusion in this book on interviewing.

Some examples of the use of observation in both consumer and industrial market research are:

■ **Respondent reactions.** The facial reaction of a respondent to a question can be telling. Looks of surprise, doubt or conviction could say as much to the interviewer as the verbal answer itself. Observation gives the interviewer the all-important 'feel' for a subject. (See also Chapter 9.)

■ **Buying practices.** Consumer market researchers can use observation to show where a store should be located. Simply standing outside the proposed location and counting the number of people that walk past could contribute to the decision. Inside a store, observation can be used to determine patterns of consumer traffic. It can show which paths they follow, which section they go to first, how they look around as they walk through the store. Business-to-business market researchers have fewer opportunities for observing the buying process. However, cash and carries, wholesalers and depots all present the chance to see customers carry out the final part of the buying transaction. The interviewer is able to see the extent to which a buyer's choice can be switched at the last minute, whether any purchases are made on impulse, and the importance of price and discounts at the point of sale.

■ **Selling practices.** Observation plays an important role in 'mystery buyer' surveys. In these, the interviewer poses as a potential buyer in order to see how the sales staff cope with a prospective customer. The interviewer measures how long it takes the salesman to begin his sales 'spiel', whether or not he describes all the features and benefits, whether a trial is offered, whether price discounts are given away before the mystery buyer has asked for them, and so on. This form of research is used extensively in the motor trade to test the effectiveness of the dealer sales network.

- **Operating procedures.** Observation can show how something is really done and not just how people say it is done. Watching how toilets are cleaned led to the development of cleaning fluid bottles with a 'swan neck', enabling the fluid to be squirted under the rim. Manufacturers of machine tools watch operators to see if they have difficulty with the controls. A manufacturer of blast cleaning equipment sent his interviewer onto sites to observe the product in use. The difficulties of manhandling the equipment led to a new design which could be easily managed by one person. In the field, the 'gun' of the blast cleaner was observed to be nozzle heavy, making it tiresome to hold and was consequently redesigned to give a better balance.
- **Stock and display.** Visits to stores, wholesalers and trade depots can be used to check on the type of displays which are used. The interviewer can see if special props and point of sale material are being used, how one store compares with another and whether the displays are positioned correctly.
- **Quality checks.** Observation plays an important role in checking on advertising posters around the country. Teams of interviewers are sent round to ensure that the correct poster is on display and that it is in good condition. The reliability of industrial products can be checked by visiting users and observing levels of wear and performance.
- **Pricing.** Shopkeepers have always used observation to check on the prices of their neighbours. Industrial researchers also use price lists to see if they are in line with the competition. However, published price lists are usually only the starting point from which discounts are given and the latter may not be published.
- **Sampling.** Sample frames for interviewing can be built up by observation. Interviewers may have to find people who drive certain types of new car. Potential respondents can be spotted very easily because their cars stand proud on their driveways. A survey to find out food manufacturers' attitudes to imported glass bottles began by sending interviewers into supermarkets to look at the jars and bottles on the shelves and record which companies packed in

glass. Observation told the researchers which companies to interview. It forewarned them which glass manufacturers the packers currently used by identifying 'punt' marks moulded into the base of every bottle.

The results of observation are recorded on conventional questionnaires, in note form, or possibly on film. A photograph can be especially useful where a record is being made of displays or the way in which something is done. Automatic cameras have obvious advantages in the hands of a field-force that is unlikely to be experienced in photography.

3

FACE-TO-FACE INTERVIEWS — WHEN AND WHERE TO USE THEM

■

Interviewing a respondent in person is the traditional and still the most common method of collecting market research data. It competes with telephone and postal research as data collection methods and has lost ground, especially to telephone interviewing, in the last few years. Nevertheless, it has a number of distinct advantages.

THE ADVANTAGES OF FACE-TO-FACE INTERVIEWING

■ Better explanations. In a personal interview, the interviewer can gain a deeper understanding of the validity of the response. In a face-to-face situation better explanations are possible as the respondents' face and hand actions are used to make points. Longer explanations are possible as there is less pressure on time, unlike someone with a telephone handset fastened to the ear. If the respondent is answering a technical point he is able to draw a diagram or use a brochure to express himself more clearly. There are many occasions, particularly associated with advertising research, when the interviewer needs to show advertisements, logos, headlines or samples. This can only be carried out in a controlled way in a face-to-face interview.

In a business-to-business survey or one that involves a few depth interviews, the interviewer's interpretation of the response could be useful. Being in the respondent's office, hearing the confidence of the answer, and seeing the premises, all help to build a picture which enables the interviewer to know if the right information is coming through.

■ **Depth.** Following on from the above point, it is easier to maintain the interest of a respondent for a longer period of time if the interview is face-to-face. The interviewer is in a better position to judge if the respondent is becoming bored or fractious. Encouragement can be given or a diversion can be made to allow a respite. Cooperation tends to be better at a personal interview. Respondents find it harder to refuse to answer questions than would be the case over the telephone or in a self-completion questionnaire. The physical presence of the interviewer seems to make the survey bona fide. Concern about confidentiality can be more readily satisfied than with an 'anonymous' person at the end of a phone. An interviewer on the doorstep or in the high street can readily show her identity card.

■ **Greater accuracy.** In a face-to-face interview the respondent has more time to reflect and consider. If required, data can be referred to, products looked at, invoices recalled or phone calls made to friends or colleagues to confirm a point. Very often the interviewer can see that the answer is correct.

■ **Product placements.** Products which are being tested can be sent through the post but it is usually better for the interviewer to deliver them by hand. In this way control is maintained over the placement so that the product arrives undamaged, advice can be given on how to use it, pre-test questions can be asked, and arrangements can be made for following up the test.

THE DISADVANTAGES OF FACE-TO-FACE INTERVIEWING

Against the advantages of face-to-face interviewing, there are a number of disadvantages:

■ **Organisation.** Face-to-face interviews are difficult to organise compared with those undertaken from a central location by phone. If the interviews are spread nationwide, a field-force covering the country is required. With a complex subject and questionnaire, a personal briefing is necessary and this is expensive, time-consuming and awkward to arrange. (There are nearly always some interviewers who cannot make the briefing and separate arrangements need to be made for them.) When the interviewing is complete, the questionnaires must be collected. There is the risk that, despite the most precise instructions, one or two inter-viewers do not return their completed questionnaires as requested and the analysis ends up a few short. Time does not usually allow for these to be repeated and, in the case of advertising studies, schedules overtake the research, pre-venting further fieldwork.

  Monitoring face-to-face interviews is much more difficult than is the case with telephone interviews. Face-to-face interviews need to have a supervisor in attendance for part of the time and check-backs, by visit or post, must be organised. For the most part, however, the interviewer is working in isolation and the quality of the work has a greater dependency on the conscientiousness of the indi-vidual. Telephone interviewing carried out from a central location and with constant supervision, eliminates these problems.

■ **Cost.** The cost of face-to-face consumer interviews varies considerably between those carried out in the street and those in the home. Household interviews that are based on pre-selected addresses are in turn more expensive than those to a quota. In general, street interviews cost the same to carry out as telephone interviews. In some cases, street interviews offer advantages by allowing show cards and visuals, while at other times the facility to random sample and achieve complete geographical coverage could swing the benefits in favour of telephone interviewing.

A comparison between face-to-face and other methods of data collection must take into consideration *all costs*. Face-to-face interviewing may use interviewers employed at the same rates as (say) telephone interviewing, but work in the field incurs expense. Allowances have to be made for bringing people together for briefings, while out-of-pocket expenses include lunches, travel, parking and post. These 'extras' will, in some cases, equal the cost of the labour.

In business-to-business market research there is no comparison between the cost of telephone and visit interviews. Visit interviews are almost always the more expensive. A face-to-face interview with a respondent in business needs a telephone discussion in advance to set it up and this, in itself, is similar in cost to a telephone interview. In business-to-business research it is not unusual to have to travel (there and back) for six or eight hours to obtain an important interview which may only last an hour. The cost of travel is enormous compared with the cost of a long-distance phone call. Normally a good average for industrial face-to-face interviews is one or two a day, though this figure could rise to four or five if they are concentrated in a conurbation. Allowing for the time taken to set up the interviews, carry them out, write up notes and make the necessary travel arrangements, visit interviews cost between five and ten times those carried out by telephone — and this is assuming that the same consultant grade interviewer does both. In reality, telephone interviews are usually carried out by specially trained staff working at lower labour rates than consultants. The savings which result from using telephone interviews are, therefore, actually much greater; sometimes less than a twentieth the cost of personal visits.

■   **Time.** Face-to-face interviews take longer to carry out because there is more adminstration required and, apart from street interviews, less can be done in a day. The inevitable prior commitments of the field-force and the delays in the postal/delivery service which is used to return the completed visit questionnaires, normally means that at least a two-week period is necessary for organising a face-to-face interviewing project. Jobs which involve many hundreds of interviews can take longer. Business-to-business fieldwork inevitably takes longer still as the interviewers struggle to set up interviews in busy managers' diaries.

4

CONSUMER FACE-TO-FACE INTERVIEWS

■

Face-to-face interviews have lost out to telephone research during the 1980s and 1990s but they still account for over half of the UK spend on research. In this chapter, consideration is given to the location of the two most important types of consumer face-to-face interview — those carried out in the street and those undertaken in the home. Other types of consumer face-to-face interviews, namely hall tests and group discussions, are the subjects of later chapters.

STREET INTERVIEWS

THE APPLICATIONS OF STREET INTERVIEWS

■ **Where the people in the street are likely to be the target group.** If the subject of the survey is food or shopping, it makes sense that the interviews are carried out close to a busy shopping area. The people who the researcher is interested in interviewing will be using the shops at some time or another. The logical places to carry out a survey of commuters is at airports, railway stations, bus stations and car parks. The commuter survey would need to have a spread of times and locations. A shopping survey should cover each day of the week including any late nights which could attract different groups (eg husbands and families). Because weekends are a busy time for shopping, these too need to be given an appropriate weighting.

■ **Where the questionnaire is short and simple.** Using a short questionnaire, and assuming that the questions are applicable for most of the passers-by, an interviewer can achieve 30 and sometimes more interviews in a day. (Interviewer days are normally six hours.)

■ **Where the questions appertain to a local issue.** A survey investigating a local issue could be suited to street interviewing. Interviewers positioned in a busy town centre would be able to collect the views of local people who are travelling to work or shopping. Clearly this would not be possible in a town with a heavy influx of tourists or visitors.

■ **Where cost and time are vital issues.** Cost should not, in theory, determine the research method. Researchers, however, learn to be pragmatists, especially where the choice is street interviews or none at all. Wherever time is in short supply, street interviews also have an advantage. They are quicker and easier to organise than house-to-house visits.

THE LIMITATIONS OF STREET INTERVIEWS

■ **Where the interview is long or complicated.** The street is not a place to carry out interviews which take more than five to ten minutes. Shoppers with their arms laden or dashing home are unlikely to be fans of the market research industry if they are stopped for more than a few minutes by an interviewer in the street.

■ **Where it is necessary to show many visuals.** It is difficult to show visuals or prompt cards in a street interview. Respondents could be caught without their glasses, the light may be poor, the rain or wind could cause problems and, if the shopper's hands are full, the show cards cannot conveniently be held.

■ **Where the targets for interview are not likely to be around.**

The street would not be the best place to obtain interviews with working people who, by definition, are likely to be at their offices or factories when the shops are open. Old people who cannot easily get about, people who are ill, and people who dislike shopping are not going to be available for interviewing in large numbers in street surveys. They probably shop at quiet times or use the corner store.

■ **Where it is necessary to calculate the accuracy of the results.** Street interviews may not provide a representative cross-section of the population. As noted above, those in full-time employment could escape the net in street interviews. It is usual, therefore, for street interviews to be carried out against a quota to ensure that all groups are included in the correct proportions. Quota samples do not allow the calculation of sampling error.

HOUSEHOLD INTERVIEWS

The advantages and disadvantages of household interviews are, by and large, the corollaries of those for street interviews. They are nevertheless worth stating to highlight the strengths and weaknesses of the method.

THE APPLICATIONS OF HOUSEHOLD INTERVIEWS

■ **Where the interview is long and complicated.** An interview of more than ten minutes needs to be carried out at the respondent's home. The interview may still be completed on the doorstep but the option exists for respondents to invite the interviewer inside and sit down if they wish. Depth interviews can only be undertaken in the home. They take between a half an hour to one hour to complete and usually require the relaxed environment which can only be found in a respondent's home.

■ **Where there are products or visuals to show.** Visuals (show cards, advertisements, storyboards) need to be shown in a convenient environment. If there are many things to show, it may be necessary to lay them out on a table, and this demands a home environment. Similarly, demonstrations of products needs to be undertaken in the home.

■ **Where a probability sampling method is used.** Random sampling demands the selection of households or people from the electoral register or by a random walk. (Probability samples can also be used with telephone interviews.)

■ **Where special addresses form the sample.** A special list of people may be used as the sample. These could be customers who have returned a guarantee card, people who have enquired about a product, or people who read certain magazines. As the sample is made up of pre-selected addresses, the interviews must be carried out at the household, although telephone interviews would also be a possibility.

■ **Where the questions are of a sensitive nature.** If the questions are personal or sensitive in any way, it is better to carry out the interview in the privacy of the respondent's home where there is no one to overhear. Sensitive questions need a careful approach. The interviewer cannot jump straight in but must ease the respondent through the questions which lead into the subject. There is not enough time for these preliminaries in street interviews.

■ **Where the interviewer needs to check out something in the house.** Research into what has been purchased may require the interviewer to actually see the product. A serial number may have to be noted, a brand name checked, or a receipt examined. If, for example, the interviewer needed a sample of people with solid fuel appliances, these could easily be identified by walking round estates looking for houses with chimneys. Owners with double glazing, cars, certain types of garage doors and burglar alarms can all be spotted from the road.

THE LIMITATIONS OF HOUSEHOLD INTERVIEWS

■ **Where time and cost are paramount.** Household interviews are time-consuming and costly to carry out. Interviewers have to find the householder in or otherwise call back a certain number of times (normally two) until successful. Expenses run high and the number of interviews which can be carried out in a day is much less than is possible in the street. If time pressures are great, the researcher may have to consider methods other than home visits.

■ **Where the home environment could influence the response.** A survey carried out in the home with teenagers on their attitude to drugs could be swayed by fear of an ear-wagging parent. Some people may not wish to discuss personal matters such as sex, politics or religion if they are in earshot of their partner. The street is a public place but in certain circumstances it can offer more privacy than the home.

OBTAINING COOPERATION AND CARRYING OUT THE INTERVIEW

Whether the interview is in the street or the home, it is usually with a complete stranger. The interviewer asks the respondent to part with time, views, facts and opinions, usually with no reward. The respondent may be busy, aggravated by a personal problem, or simply wish to remain private and uninterrupted. The interviewer has no rights whatsoever to demand that the respondent should help. Everything depends, therefore, on the interviewer's approach.

The first few seconds are critical: it is then that the interview is won or lost. At the same time, the interviewer must be both assumptive and courteous. Respondents must be made to feel that they are being asked to do something which is important and that they are in the hands of an expert. If the interviewer has an identity card or a letter of authority, it should be shown to the respondent as part of the introduction. In a large survey, the interviewers may be given their opening lines. They will say that help is requested for a survey, which company is carrying out the survey (note that the research agency is named even though the sponsor is not revealed), and the length of time the interview can be expected to take.

MRS

The Market Research Society

Survey Interviewer Identity Card 1992	AFFIX PHOTO HERE
This Authority is only valid until 31 December 1992.	MRS Serial No: **13593**
Authorisation: *[signature]* **Peter Mouncey** *Chairman* The Market Research Society	Interviewer Name: Interviewer No: Signature:

BUSINESS & MARKET RESEARCH PLC

Business & Market Research plc
The Court, High Lane, Stockport, Cheshire SK6 8DX
Telephone: (0663) 765115

This interview is part of GENUINE research and does NOT involve selling in any way.

It is conducted under the Code of Conduct of The Market Research Society.

THIS CODE GUARANTEES THE FOLLOWING:

1 (a) Your identity will remain confidential to the organisation conducting the survey.

(b) You will not suffer any adverse effects from this contact.

(c) You are able to refuse, or withdraw from any interview at any stage.

2 Children under the age of 14 will not be approached for an interview without the permission of a parent or responsible adult (ie, teacher).

You will be given a thank-you leaflet stating the identity of the organisation carrying out the survey at the end of the interview.

If you have any queries, please contact the MRS or the organisation carrying out the survey.

Card issued by and property of:

**The Market Research Society, 15 Northburgh Street, London EC1V 0AH
Telephone: 071-490 4911**

Figure 4.1 Interviewer's identity card

The interviewer must expect rejections. However, it is usually possible to overcome the fears and objections of the respondents. People who are busy, who are harassed or feel the need to maintain their privacy, could have important views or buying characteristics which would make a valuable contribution to the survey.

Objections fall into a pattern and can be pre-empted:

■ **The respondent who has no time.** The interviewer must make a judgement on this. It is unreasonable to expect a shopper who is running for a bus to miss it for the sake of a survey. However, many people will use the excuse of not having time as a let-out. Respondents will make the time if they are interested in the survey. A boring subject is not an easy hurdle for the interviewer to overcome and it becomes necessary to fall back on every ounce of enthusiasm and persuasion to get the respondent to cooperate. Where the sample consists of pre-selected addresses, the interviewer may have to arrange to return at a more convenient time.

■ **The respondent believes they can't answer the questions.** Some respondents see market research interviews as tests. They worry that they will give the wrong answer or make a fool of themselves. A good interviewer soon becomes skilled at alleviating any concerns the respondent may have.

■ **The respondent who values privacy.** The higher up the social grades and income levels, the more 'difficult' respondents can become. Their egos and sense of importance or their genuine wish for privacy can be expressed brusquely. The interviewer must hope to be able to persuade these people that the data from surveys is one of the most important ways in which manufacturers and suppliers ensure that they are offering what the public wants. An assurance must be given that the information will be pooled to draw conclusions and that there is no way that the responses of individuals can be tied to any one person. It should be stressed that the survey is for market research purposes only and will not be followed up by a sales approach.

The interviewer should act positively and lead with the first question as soon as possible. Once the respondent becomes involved and interested in the questions, cooperation has been won. Very few respondents abandon an interview once they have started.

Keeping the pace of the interview going is important. Ironically, it is the respondents who claim to be too busy or short of time who are the ones who are difficult to keep on track during questioning. Respondents who stray from the questions or who find it difficult to be straightforward in their replies must be guided firmly through the interview. If the interview is lengthy the interviewer can help by giving encouragement or saying when the end is in sight.

If there are a lot of classification questions, they are usually left until last. The respondent has, one hopes, got into the swing of cooperating by this time and will not worry unduly about saying what occupation is held by the head of the household, the age of the housewife and the number of children in the family. Classification questions are important to researchers as they enable the results to be analysed by grouping and contrasting different types of people. There is, however, a disturbing trend in the research industry to throw into a survey as many classification questions as possible in case they prove useful. This is not helpful in generating respondent sympathy and cooperation as the relevance of the classification questions is often tenuous at best.

On completion, the interviewer owes the respondent a thank-you. Sometimes a card is given to the respondent which explains who carried out the interview and why. In street interviews it is normal practice for the interviewer to ask the respondent for their name and address. This is used to carry out a check-back on a percentage of the interviews (usually 10 per cent) to ensure the work was carried out satisfactorily. Diplomacy and a special explanation may be needed for some people who are reticent about giving their address to a stranger.

The interview may be complete but the interviewer has not finished. A final check is needed over the basic details. All questions should be legible and answered (or marked as a refusal). The name of the interviewer, the date, and the respondent's name and

Business & Market Research plc

MARKETING CONSULTANTS

BUXTON ROAD, HIGH LANE VILLAGE, STOCKPORT, CHESHIRE SK6 8DX
TELEPHONE (0663) 765115   FAX (0663) 762362

Thank you for helping with this market research project by letting us interview you.

When we are doing research such as this, people ask many questions about how and why we conduct it. We thought it would be helpful to provide the answers to some of these questions.

Q. *Why was I asked to help?*

A. On most research jobs we have to talk with a cross-section of the public. People from all walks of life, and all ages. We have to talk with people who either have something specific, like a colour TV; or have done something special like having a holiday in a particular place or country. Sometimes people are asked to help because they live in a particular place. All of this is to make sure that the people whose opinions we collect, are representative of the rest of the population.

Q. *How can I be sure that someone is a genuine Market Researcher?*

A. (1) Ask to see his/her identity card.

   (2) Ring the telephone number at the bottom of the page overleaf.

   (3) Contact the Market Research Society and ask if they know of the company the interviewer is working for.

Q. *Are people trained to do interviewing?*

A. YES.
   Interviewers are carefully selected and professionally trained.

Q. *Why bother to do Market Research at all?*

A. With over 55 million people living in this country it is necessary to find out what they want from the things they buy. What sizes, shapes, design they should be: what TV programmes we like etc. So it is necessary to ask the people who buy or use or need these things for their views. This way, if things are wrong, or just 'not quite right' we can tell the manufacturer, government department, business, or TV companies what their customers think. They can then improve their goods, services or programmes and provide what the public needs.

BUSINESS
& MARKET
RESEARCH PLC

Q. *Why do you want my name and address?*

A. So a small percentage of the people who help on a survey will get either a letter or a phone call (or perhaps are called on again) from a Supervisor of the company. This call or letter will be to thank you again for your help and find out if you were happy with the interview. We are then able to tell our clients that we contacted a percentage of the people interviewed and all was well. No-one outside the company doing the survey is ever allowed to know your name and address. Because we don't give our clients names of the people who help us we have to prove to our clients that an interviewer really did call on you and did do an interview with you.

Finally, we would like to thank you once again for sparing some of your time to help us.

We hope that the answers to these questions have helped to explain a little of what we do.

If you have any further questions or worries, or comments, please contact either the company named at the bottom of this page or the Market Research Society.

This leaflet is produced by the Market Research Society who have a Code of Conduct that its members adhere to.

The Code of Conduct states that the principles on which respondents' protection is based are:

(a) by having assurances honoured.

(b) by being allowed to remain anonymous

(c) by avoiding adverse effects from the contact

(d) by being able to refuse or withdraw from an interview at any stage

(e) by being able to check the credentials of the interviewer.

Interviewed by ....

The Market Research Society
15 Northburgh Street London EC1V 0AH
Tel: 071-490 4911   Fax: 071-490 0608

Figure 4.2   Thank you card

address should be checked to ensure that they are filled in. Finally the completed questionnaires and any other material that needs to be returned to the office should be parcelled up for despatch. The postal instructions should be carefully followed. The field-force administration at the office is unlikely to believe stories of recorded delivery or registered post slips which disappear along with a batch of questionnaires — they have heard these excuses too often.

5

BUSINESS-TO-BUSINESS FACE-TO-FACE INTERVIEWS

■

TYPES OF BUSINESS-TO-BUSINESS FACE-TO-FACE INTERVIEW

Business-to-business face-to-face interviews can be classified as one of three types:

■ **Structured interviews.** These are similar in most respects to consumer interviews where the interviewer faithfully follows the structure of the questions as laid out in the questionnaire. Most structured questionnaires have closed questions in which the respondents' answers are forced into one of a number of predetermined codes. The format is rigid in that the interviewer has no discretion to stray from either the wording of the questions or their order. Structured interviews are used in large fieldwork programmes where it is essential that each and every interview is comparable. They are not suited to surveys where there are subtle differences between the respondents. There is nothing more infuriating for a respondent than to have his answer forced into a response category that he knows is not quite right.

■ **Semi-structured interviews.** In these interviews a questionnaire is still used but there are many open-ended questions and the interviewer has more latitude to administer it in a way that suits the respondent. This could involve probing for explanations or skipping questions which are obviously not relevant. The flexibility of semi-structured interviews makes them very popular in business-to-business market research, especially for technical surveys. However, interviewers need a high level of skills to be able to cope with a changing situation in each interview.

■ **Unstructured interviews.** The third type of business-to-business interview is known as 'in-depth' or 'unstructured', as the questions are more in the form of a check list of topics than a formal questionnaire. (See also Chapter 9.) The free-ranging discussion which takes place is rewarding to both the interviewer and the respondent. It is, however, the most difficult type of interview to control, requiring knowledge and confidence on the part of the interviewer if the cooperation of the respondent is to be maintained. The interviewer must be prepared to enter avenues of interest opened up in the discussion as there is a high level of spontaneity which is sparked off by points raised during the interview. The interview can only be successfully administered by an experienced market research consultant.

OBTAINING THE INTERVIEW

The business-to-business interviewer faces different problems from his consumer counterpart in obtaining the cooperation of respondents. Business-to-business interviews are almost always held in the respondent's place of work. The interview is planned and scheduled for a specific time, so there are no problems associated with the shopper confronted in the street or the householder disturbed by a knock on the door. The business-to-business respondent is, however, almost certain to be busy. If time is given during working hours, it is at the company's expense and the respondent may need to work harder to make up for the lost time. Respondents may be uncertain of whether they are vested with the authority to answer the questions and be concerned as to whether any replies give away commercial secrets. If the interviewer cannot disclose the sponsor of the study, this could be a valid concern.

The interviewer must rely on powers of persuasion and salesmanship in order to obtain cooperation. There is little to offer the respondent except the nebulous promise of better products and service at some future date. In the interviewer's favour is the interest that people have in their jobs. Most people are flattered at being given the opportunity to talk about their work, the suppliers they use and how and why they choose them.

The interviewer must have worked out an introduction before making contact with the respondent. Absolute confidence and assurance must be displayed in the initial approach. Even so, there will be rejections:

- It is company policy not to take part in surveys.
- We have already taken part in a survey recently.
- I'm too busy right now. Try me again in a few weeks.
- I'm not the person you want to speak to.
- We only do questionnaires through the post. Send it to me and I'll complete it for you.
- You'll have to give me an idea of the questions before I can help you.
- What's in it for me?
- I know the research sponsor and I've told him all that I have to say on the subject.

For more details on overcoming objections, see Chapter 10.

There are a number of guidelines which will head off any objections and help the business-to-business researcher achieve cooperation:

- **Be brief.** The interviewer should come straight to the point. The respondent will become bored with a long-winded introduction and, in any case, it provides the time to dream up plenty of objections.
- **Be honest.** The interviewer is not trying to sell something and the respondent should be assured that this is the case.

To purport to be representing some spurious company or purpose is unethical, to say the least. Clients should be persuaded, if at all possible, to allow the interviewer to disclose their name as the study sponsor. Very often they wish to remain anonymous because of a fear that competitors will be able to take advantage of the knowledge that they are behind a survey. In fact, there is little that any competitor can do with such information. Being able to state who the interviewer is working for helps cooperation enormously. After all, if respondents ask only one question, it is likely to be 'who is the research sponsored by?'. If this question is rebuffed by the interviewer at the time of seeking the interview, it does little to help.

■ **Justify the study.** The respondent wants to hear that the study is important and could have some benefit for himself and his company. The promise of better service, improved designs or better quality could help rationalize why it is worth spending time answering questions.

■ **Give assurances.** The interviewer should assure the respondent that the information will be confidential to the research department or agency. It may help to provide this assurance in writing. It may also be necessary to alleviate any fears about the difficulty of the questions with reassurances that they are sure to be within the respondent's experience.

■ **Confirm the interview.** As a courtesy to the respondent, but also to ensure there is no confusion about the date and time of the interview, the researcher should confirm the arrangements by letter or fax.

CONDUCTING THE INTERVIEW

At the interview, the respondent is playing host but expects the initiative to be taken by his guest. At the outset it is worth the interviewer recapping the purpose of the survey and how the respondent is expected to help. Any assurances of confidentiality should be repeated.

The interview begins with simple background questions. Establishing the history of the respondent's company and the development of the market are useful questions which will warm the respondent to the task. When a relaxed environment has been created the interviewer can use the questionnaire to guide the discussion.

The respondent is anticipating being asked questions and the interviewer need not be coy about it. The clipboard, questionnaire and tape recorder should be brought out straight away. It is self-delusion to believe that the interview can be carried out without taking notes. The interviewer should write anything and everything down from the very beginning: the respondent will expect it.

Taping interviews does not induce the inhibitions which might be imagined. An assumptive and confident manner works best, perhaps introducing the tape recorder as an 'electronic notebook' to compensate for slow writing skills. The respondent will soon forget it is there.

At the end of the interview, deliberately putting away the clip board or turning off the tape recorder should completely remove any remaining tension and provide the opportunity to ask, as an aside, those all-important delicate questions. The responses can then be noted down as soon as the interviewer is out of the office.

Face-to-face interviews have the big advantage of providing the opportunity for clarification and going back over technical answers. If the interviewer is unclear or suspects that a misunderstanding has occurred, the question can be asked again in a different way. For example, the respondent may have trouble providing an answer regarding the size of the market because this subject has never been considered in those terms. However, the respondent may feel able to make a sensible guess at his own company's share of the market and, knowing the turnover of the company, it is a simple matter to calculate the market size. By thinking laterally, the interviewer can find ways of making it easier for the respondent to answer the questions.

Respondents do not know the degree of precision to which the interviewer is working. Usually an approximation is better than no answer at all. Thus, the respondent who claims not to know the purchases of a product may actually be saying that he doesn't know them in detail without a good deal of sifting through computer printouts. A prompt from the interviewer could put an order of magnitude to the purchases: 'Were they more than one million units per year?'. The answer can be refined until it is as close to the respondent's knowledge as possible without going to considerably more trouble.

Finally, there are the respondents who give vague answers, requiring the interviewer to use probing questions to find out what is going on. Typical responses which need following with a probe are:

- They are best/worst.
- Because we've always done it this way.
- I think they are good/bad.
- I like/dislike them.
- Because we expect our purchases to grow/decline.

At the end of the interview the researcher must close and thank the respondent and make a note to follow up any promises made in reciprocation. The door should be left open to go back for clarification should it be required when the data is being analysed. A thank-you letter costs little in time and money and will help to ensure that the interviewer (or a colleague) will be cordially received at some future date.

6

TELEPHONE INTERVIEWS — WHEN AND WHERE TO USE THEM

■

THE ROLE OF TELEPHONE INTERVIEWING

Telephone interviewing is the most widely used method of field-work in business-to-business market research. Furthermore, with the exception of postal surveys, all other forms of fieldwork in business-to-business research involve initial telephone contact such as making visit appointments, inviting respondents to group discussions and clinics and so on. Telephone interviewing is also used increasingly in consumer market research, finding favour over street and household interviews.

ADVANTAGES OF TELEPHONE INTERVIEWING

The greatest advantages of the telephone are its speed and low cost. These are most evident in business-to-business market research.

A sample of industrial establishments (such as chemical plants, printers, wholesalers or whatever) is always geographic-ally dispersed and if visits are the selected method, unproductive time is lost in travelling. In favourable circumstances, perhaps four 30-minute interviews of a similar type can be completed in a day while the rest of the time is spent travelling between companies, parking, walking round the building etc. In reality the number of interviews per day will be somewhat less because time will have been spent on the phone setting them up. By contrast, at least ten 20-minute interviews could be completed by telephone during the day. The cost difference between visits and telephone interviews, therefore, reflects primarily the greater productivity of the latter and also the fact that telephone charges are considerably less than travel costs.

Over and above the time and cost advantages, telephone interviewing is a very practical means of data collection. In fact, such may be the constraints of time and cost that any other type of primary research might be impossible.

In consumer research the time and cost advantages are not quite so clear-cut. If the comparison is between street and telephone interviewing then there is probably little difference in either time or cost — and street interviewing might even be the cheaper. However, the telephone is both quicker and cheaper than household interviews since time is not wasted in travel between interview points.

A strong argument in favour of telephone interviewing in business-to-business market research is that virtually anyone targeted for interview will be on the phone. The only exception is the construction industry, where building sites are either not on the phone or are difficult to trace.

In contrast, not all households have a phone. Currently 85 per cent of homes in the UK are on the phone but this still leaves 15 per cent of households who would be left out of any research conducted solely by telephone. In fact, the proportion eliminated from a consumer telephone survey is far greater than this as a fifth of the people on the phone are ex-directory.

Nor is the phone wholly accepted as a medium for carrying out interviews as is the case in business. Business-to-business respondents accept the phone as part and parcel of their daily lives while to many a householder it is an intrusion into their resting or social hours.

Conversely, security fears are working in favour of the telephone as an interviewing medium. Householders are saved the worry of answering the door to a stranger while interviewers themselves are not exposed to the risks of entering dubious neighbourhoods.

THE ARGUMENTS AGAINST THE USE OF TELEPHONE INTERVIEWS

We have seen that there are a number of strong arguments in favour of telephone interviews, with particularly important benefits in cost and speed. However, there are sometimes good reasons for *not* using telephone interviews.

VISUALS ARE DIFFICULT TO USE

It is possible, though something of an inconvenience, to arrange to show visuals to a respondent who is interviewed by telephone. The fax or post allows information to be sent but it cannot be 'unfolded' in the same way as is possible when face-to-face. This limitation may rule out the telephone as a tool in new product research where, without showing either the product or an illustration, it cannot be adequately described. (Even if a satisfactory verbal description can be devised it may prove too long and complex to convey over the phone.) Similarly, the inability to be able to show logo styles or banners of newspapers and journals may create difficulties in using the telephone in brand recognition or readership surveys.

If a product or a visual *has* to be shown then the telephone is not the right approach. However, telephone interviews may still have a role to play, feeding in information to a wider project. For example, in new product research, data on current methods of using or consuming products may be required and this could be obtained over the telephone satisfactorily, leaving face-to-face interviews specifically to test the new concept.

With some imagination, means can be devised of carrying out

interviews using more than one approach such as phone/fax/ phone or phone/letter/phone. By splitting the interview in this way the researcher can obtain up to an hour of respondents' time without taxing their patience at one sitting *and at a substantially lower cost than through visits.*

PROMPTED QUESTIONS

It is sometimes necessary to ask respondents to consider a number of pre-determined factors in order to find out which they identify with, which they have used, which reflects their way of doing things and so on. More than five or six factors on a list are difficult to retain in the mind and so it is usual to show these on a card in order that they can be given fair consideration.

One way of overcoming this limitation of communicating a long list of factors over the phone is to ask respondents to write down the points. This takes time, it requires pen and paper to be at hand, and it assumes respondents will cooperate and do as they are asked.

Questions in which statements or brands are rated can be tedious when administered over the phone, especially if they are highly repetitive. A solution is to ask the questions as scores out of five where five is very good and one is very poor. Once the respondent has grasped this simple concept it becomes easier to ask whole series of questions without labouring through verbiage.

UNCONSIDERED RESPONSES

The telephone abhors silence and this forces instant responses to questions. On many occasions this does not matter and, indeed, the instant response may be the one which is best. For example, the first brand name which comes to mind, or the key strength of a company may be the answer which is sought. However, it can be unrealistic to expect a respondent to always give a meaningful response 'off the top of the head'. Consider the following:

■   What make of car do you normally drive?

■   How many pads of writing paper does your company use
      in a year?

It can reasonably be expected that most people could give an
instant response to the first question. In the second case, however, it can be assumed that most respondents are unlikely to be
able to give an accurate, instant response as they just do not have
that type of information available. Nor will the information be to
hand if the interviewer is face-to-face with the respondent (but at
least there is a chance that the answer can be worked out).

The solution to the problem is usually to reconsider the question. In the example just mentioned, it might be better to ask
about the monthly use of writing pads or about order frequency
or typical size of orders, thus allowing the interviewer to derive a
figure for the annual consumption.

INTERVIEW LENGTH

Telephone interviewing is, on the whole, better suited to shorter
interviews and 10 to 15 minutes or so is probably the ideal length.
Visit interviews are usually longer and in business-to-business
situations, a visit interview of less than half an hour would probably
be regarded as too short to justify the trouble.

This limitation of telephone interviewing is, however, a matter
of degree. Longer interviews can be carried out on the phone
when the subject is engaging or if the interviewer is skilled at
keeping the respondent going. The quality of the questionnaire
also plays an important part as a well designed questionnaire will
draw the respondent along without any perception as to how long
they have actually been on the phone.

INTERVIEW DEPTH

In telephone interviews the questions and answers are generally
kept short and so the medium is not ideal for depth interviewing.
The pressure on time means that respondents avoid long and discursive responses. Furthermore, the lack of personal contact

means that the interviewer is unable to assess the responses and obtain that extra feel for the accuracy of the reply as is possible in a face-to-face situation.

Undoubtedly there is truth in all these points but again, this difference between the telephone and visits is one of degree. Even in visits, simple questions are usually preferable to more complex ones. There are still time constraints and without skilful prompting, respondents may limit themselves to the simple, short response. Also, in large-scale visit interview programmes, many of the qualitative insights obtained in the interviews are either not recorded adequately or prove difficult to incorporate in the formal analysis of the data. Furthermore, in face-to-face interviewing, that all-important element of control is missing as the work is done out of sight (albeit there is a 10 per cent random check on each interviewer's work). This compares with telephone interviews which are carried out under supervision from a central unit.

In conclusion there are circumstances where the telephone interview is less suitable, or even totally unsuitable, than a visit, and therefore is completely ruled out. However, recognizing and accepting these limitations, the application of telephone interviewing is still enormous and, with exceptions such as new product research, covers most areas likely to be relevant in a project.

7

CARRYING OUT EFFECTIVE TELEPHONE INTERVIEWS

■

We now turn to practical advice on carrying out a programme of telephone interviewing — how to plan and achieve successful interviews over the phone.

PLANNING

The important subject of questionnaire design is covered in another book in this series. Suffice to say here that a well-planned and well-structured questionnaire is even more important for telephone use than for a visit. The interviewer must be able to put the questions fluently, ensure the questions which are asked are meaningful and that they follow an effective sequence. The questionnaire designed for the telephone should have simple and straightforward questions, in other words, it should be designed to suit the medium.

Where more than one interviewer is to work on a telephone project, a formal briefing session is needed with the background to the research outlined and the questionnaire worked through in detail. Interviewers must be totally familiar with the questions before attempting the first interview. However, in this respect, telephone and visit interviewing are no different.

In telephone interviewing, a directory of one kind or another may be used to obtain the sample. In the case of consumer research, the 'white pages' of the telephone directories are an excellent frame from which to choose the random sample. However, some points should be borne in mind about using the telephone directory in this way.

- The telephone directory is not a comprehensive list of all subscribers. It excludes new connections and, probably more significantly, 'ex-directory' subscribers who may form a significant element of a particular group and may, therefore, introduce an unquantifiable level of bias. This can be overcome by a form of random dialling. A sample of phone numbers is randomly selected but each number is then increased by 1 (eg 5115 becomes 5116). The sample should now be a near random sample of subscribers.

- The directory is best regarded as a list of households than of individuals and an additional procedure will be needed to select individual respondents within a home, eg quotas by sex and household status.

- Until contact is made, nothing is known about the respondents at the other end of the line. This may mean a high ratio of contacts to interviews if the respondent has to qualify by, for example, ownership of a particular product or having some personal characteristic. In contrast, face-to-face interviewing may enable some contact wastage to be avoided. If gardeners are to be interviewed about lawn care products, then the face-to-face interviewer knows there is little point approaching houses with no gardens. Via the telephone this is not obvious. Similarly, if the sample sought is females over 40, an interviewer in the street would be able to select appropriate respondents through observation. The telephone prohibits these vital initial screens.

It is desirable, in telephone interviewing, to keep contact sheets which provide a record of all calls made (rather than just successful interviews). At the end of interviewing these contact sheets show who did *not* qualify for interview or who refused or where a respondent was not available. Thus, the analysis of the contact sheets helps cost and plan future work and it provides information which may be relevant to the findings of the survey itself. The layout of the contact sheets can be designed to meet the needs of specific jobs but the usual format is a line for each contact and columns to record the outcome of calls.

Job Number:	Project Name:					
Respondent's name	Address	Date/time of calling			Result	
		1st call	2nd call	3rd call	Interview (tick)	Reason for non-interview

Figure 7.1 Example of contact sheet

Another important type of record is the *costs incurred*, specifically the telephone charges. These costs may have to be accounted for and charged to a client. Even if this is not the case, reasonably accurate costings are desirable (for budgeting future work, for example).

Telephone costs are based on time and call bands related to distance, therefore costs can be calculated by timing each call and multiplying by the appropriate rate. Costing in this way is, however, a chore and, if telephone interviewing on any scale is undertaken, it is far better to have meters fitted to the phones. These cost little and automatically record the units used per call or per interviewing session.

A final aspect of planning telephone interviews is setting call objectives — that is the number of interviews which should be achieved in a day. A realistic objective depends on the following factors:

- The nature of the respondents and the difficulty of contacting them. If it is necessary to interview respondents who are only available at particular times, the strike rate will be less than for respondents who are always at their desk. Farmers, for example, are away from a phone for most of their working day and are perhaps most easily interviewed early in the morning, at lunchtime or early evening. Dentists, on the other hand, are in the surgery ten hours or more a day but are perhaps only available for interview for half an hour during that time. People in business are always in meetings!

- Respondent's qualification for interview. If respondents have to meet very specific qualifications before they can be interviewed, this will cut back the number of interviews which can be achieved per day. In consumer research, for example, the respondent may have to own or buy a certain product or fall within a particular demographic grouping.

- Interview duration — that is whether they are going to take ten minutes or half an hour once a suitable respondent has been found.

TELEPHONE MANNERS

In a telephone interview the respondent is asked to give up time and part with information to an unknown person at the end of a line. The interviewer's success in this situation depends very much on their approach.

A successful approach starts before even picking up the phone; the interviewer must adopt a positive manner. Here are a few suggestions:

- Resolve to *project a positive attitude*. Make it sound as though you want the respondent to talk to you. Any hesitancy will come across as tentative and the respondent will be far more likely to be unhelpful.
- Similarly, *sound interested in the project*. Perhaps the subject matter in the research is pretty pedestrian, if not downright boring, but this should not be allowed to transmit to the respondent. If you don't sound interested, how can you expect cooperation?
- *Don't talk too quickly*. In your initial nervousness you may be tempted to speak quickly so that the interview is completed as quickly as possible. This is counter-productive.
- *Be courteous*. Telephone interviewing can be frustrating and by the end of an exhausting day there could be a temptation to let fly at an awkward respondent who won't help and is unpleasant. It is important to rise above this and not to reply in kind; remember it is you who wants to take up someone else's time and it is their prerogative to refuse.
- *Stick to the questionnaire*. You should be using a questionnaire, however simple the interview. Stick to the questionnaire and commit to asking *all* the questions. This applies even if you designed the questionnaire.
- Using a questionnaire means *listening* to the respondent as well as asking the questions. Never finish a sentence for respondents or assume you know what they are about to say.

CONTACTING THE RIGHT RESPONDENT

The interview will only be worthwhile if the respondent is appropriate and qualified. Who should be interviewed will have been decided at the planning stage and it is only now, at the time of interviewing, that the problem becomes one of actually finding these respondents.

In consumer research the problem is usually not very acute. The target respondent may be any adult, with equal quotas of men and women. Alternatively, the respondents may have to own or have bought something, but this will be resolved through the initial questions. In either case, finding the relevant respondent is not difficult once the contact has been made.

The situation is more problematical in business-to-business market research. Generally, the respondent is defined in terms of their responsibility for some function or activity, for example, the person responsible for choosing the make of trucks in the company's fleet, or the person with day-to-day responsibility for the computer's operation.

Often these responsibilities can be equated with a specific *job title*; in the examples above perhaps the transport manager and data processing manager. However, job titles vary widely between companies. In some cases the specific responsibility may be that of a manager with wide interests, whereas in others it may be delegated downwards. In practice, therefore, the job title may be only a guide to locating the appropriate respondent and as soon as possible their specific responsibility should be checked by 'qualifying' questions, such as: 'Who decides the make of vehicles used by your company?'

Another problem in business-to-business market research is that most respondents are reached through a receptionist. Quite often receptionists do not know who in their company is responsible for a specific function and, anxious to get rid of the caller as quickly as possible, connect to the wrong person. Therefore it is better generally to ask for someone by job title and, if necessary, be prepared to go through two or more potential respondents before finding the right one.

Some other points about dealing with receptionists are:

■ As well as asking for the 'transport manager' (or whoever), ask for the person's name before being put through. This means that the respondent can be addressed personally from the outset of the interview.

■ It is better not to discuss *in any detail* with other people the reasons for wanting to speak to a respondent. Too much knowledge about the questions which lie in store may cause the receptionist to decide that the respondent does not 'want to be bothered' by a market research enquiry.

With respondents in senior management positions, the interviewer may have to hurdle a secretary whose job includes making sure the boss is not pestered with trivial phone calls. In this situation skill and politeness are the essential ingredients of getting through to the respondent. Secretaries can become strong allies in winning the interview if they are treated as important and responsible people and are taken into the confidence of the interviewer.

INITIAL CONTACT WITH THE RESPONDENT

Generally, respondents decide whether or not they are going to cooperate within the first minute of the contact. The opening gambit is therefore vital. Once through to the respondent it is important to make it clear, succinctly, that this is a market research exercise and will not result in any sales pressure.

> Hello Mr Jones. This is xxx. I am trying to find out what people think of various types of heavy trucks and I wondered if you would be kind enough to spare me a few minutes.

With a simple introduction such as this, many respondents will be willing to cooperate without further discussion and it is possible to move on to the first question. Not all respondents can be won over so easily and the interviewer must be ready to meet their objections. Suggestions for countering objections are given in Chapter 10.

DURING THE INTERVIEW

Once a respondent has agreed to go ahead, things usually get better. It is uncommon for a respondent to return to any objections or to end the interview prematurely.

During the interview it is the interviewers job to keep the respondent on course. Firmly and politely the interviewer should keep the initiative, returning to the questions, but on no account skipping questions because the respondent has half covered them in the general discussion.

The temptation to miss out questions because the respondent is showing signs of impatience must be avoided. Try to regain the respondent's interest and provide encouragement and assurances that their responses are valuable.

Where necessary, it is legitimate to depart from the script of the questionnaire to indicate that the interview is nearing the end. Normally the questions are asked as written but additional non-committal comments at the end of responses can be used as acknowledgment. These are the pleasantries which lubricate general conversation:

■ Oh, yes.
■ Yes, thank you.
■ Right.

As an aid to solving the problems presented by occasional difficult respondents, Table 7.1 shows a 'rogues' typology' and action guide suggesting means of dealing with them. Most respondents, however, more or less fall into a 'no problem' category.

AT THE END OF THE INTERVIEW

The objective at the end of the interview should be to leave the respondent as happy as possible without any regrets for having helped. If the respondent feels disgruntled and that he has been 'tricked' into participating, he will probably react negatively in future encounters with market research. In the long run, all market researchers are dependent on continuing cooperation. Also it may be necessary to go back to the respondent to check out some points at the time the data is being analysed.

Here are a few suggestions on how to finish the interview in the best way:

■ As you reach the last or next to last question, indicate that this is the case. The respondent can start to relax before the final sign off.

TABLE 7.I STRATEGIES FOR DEALING WITH DIFFICULT RESPONDENTS

Type of respondent	Characteristics	How to deal with respondents	What to avoid
Disagreeable	Wants to argue. Makes unreasonable demands. Talks loudly and abruptly. Is sarcastic and antagonistic.	Let the respondent talk — you listen. Be calm and good-natured. Try to allay any fears and get the respondent to co-operate.	Don't argue. Don't let sarcastic remarks disturb you.
Inattentive	Has 'far away' tone in his voice. Is not listening.	Be alert and full of 'pep'.	Don't allow your own attention to be distracted.
Silent	Won't answer questions. Is either tired, suspicious or has language difficulty.	Be friendly and interested. Re-state questions and ensure respondent has understood.	Don't just repeat questions in louder tone.
Talkative	Continues to talk, discusses personal affairs instead of questions.	Listen sympathetically but switch conversation back to questionnaire as soon as possible.	Don't be led into discussion of your or his personal affairs. Don't act impatiently.
Indecisive	Can't make up his mind about answers, or frightened to answer question.	Boost ego and encourage him to answer question by explaining what the purpose of the research is. Ensure question is understood.	Don't accept 'Don't know' as an answer. Try to get the respondent to give a meaningful answer to the question.

Type of respondent	Characteristics	How to deal with respondents	What to avoid
Positive	Tries to display own knowledge. Criticizes your questions etc. May be argumentative.	Welcome his opinions and ideas. Be patient, calm and attentive.	Don't argue or disagree. Don't get excited or appear intimidated.
Hurried	Appears impatient, nervous, fidgety, is brisk in manner.	Explain how long the interview will take and ask permission to proceed. Be as quick as possible or ask to call back.	Don't try to rush too much. Ensure all the questions are answered.
Deliberate	Wants time to think question over. Is slow and leisurely in speech. Appears to have unlimited time.	Get through questionnaire as efficiently as possible. Give encouragement when slow to answer.	Don't force the respondent. Don't appear hurried or impatient and don't lose interest.

■ Thank the respondent:
'Thank you Mr xxx. That is all I wanted to ask you. Your comments have been very useful.'
■ Reassure the respondent that he has participated in a market research survey and that his responses will be used for that purpose only:
'This is a market research survey and the information you have given me will not be used for any other purpose.'

When the interview is finished, quickly check over the questionnaire. In the heat of the moment, responses are often scribbled down and it is better to tidy up immediately. In particular make sure that:

■ the name of the respondent, his company (if business-to-business market research) and the telephone number are all recorded;

■ all the responses for 'closed' questions are unambiguously recorded. Where the question calls for a single response, check there is only one;

■ any 'shorthand' used to record open-ended questions is expanded to a full and legible record;

■ the units of any value recorded (eg weights, dimensions), where relevant, are clearly stated.

Checking over the questionnaires in this way can save a lot of problems later on.

COMPUTER AIDED TELEPHONE INTERVIEWING

The PC can play a role in interviewing. Interviews carried out by telephone can be guided by a questionnaire which is displayed on the screen of a computer as opposed to being on paper. The interviewer records answers by tapping numbers of the keyboard which correspond with the pre-coded responses displayed on the screen. The interviewer does not need to be concerned with routeing instructions (ie the instructions which show the next question to be asked) as with a paper based questionnaire: this is automatically catered for by the computer which skips through to the appropriate question if a certain response is received.

Screen based data entry is normally referred to as CATI, an acronym for Computer Aided Telephone Interviewing. It offers considerable advantages when the conditions are right for its use:

■ The interviewer is left free to concentrate on the interview itself as the routeing instructions are taken care of.

■ Data is entered directly and so it eliminates the extra transactions of punching (subsequent data entry). A potential source of error is, therefore, removed and costs are reduced by the elimination of the task.

- The whole exercise is speeded up because data is entered straight away.
- At intervals during the survey, the researcher can dip into the analysis and see how the results look. It can be used in this way to monitor the results and cut off the interviewing if consistent results are being achieved.

However, there are disadvantages to CATI interviewing. Coping with open-ended responses is difficult. There are systems which can accommodate these but they require good typing skills on the part of the interviewing team. If a respondent makes changes to an earlier answer when half-way through an interview, it is more difficult to return and make alterations than is the case with paper questionnaires. In general, CATI is best suited to very structured questionnaires carried out in large numbers, especially repeat surveys where all the possible answers have been worked out. Responses should be simple and straightforward, otherwise the CATI system can become inhibiting.

8

SPLIT INTERVIEWS

In Chapter 6 some limitations of telephone interviews were discussed, including the problem of not being able to show visuals. The split interview is a means of overcoming many of these limitations without the cost or timetable needed for visits. A split interview consists of an initial telephone interview, a fax or mailout of relevant material and then a follow-up telephone interview.

APPLICATIONS OF SPLIT INTERVIEWS

Split interviewing can be used to meet a range of research requirements. The technique is particularly suitable for interviews which would take too long by phone or those where it is necessary for the respondent to see something in hard copy. As discussed, pure telephone research is often inappropriate because the product cannot be shown, but with split interviewing a descriptive sheet and illustration can be faxed or posted to respondents and this may convey adequate information. If the product is small, actual samples can sometimes be mailed. Many consumer products can be handled in this way such as packets of dried foods, cleaning products, toiletries etc. Sometimes industrial products can be mailed as well, for example wiping materials or small components. However, if the product is large it probably cannot be shown, even in a visit.

As well as new products or new product data sheets, other information can be mailed to respondents prior to re-interview. In some product areas, for example, it may be difficult to define product classifications adequately over the phone. A mailed data sheet, probably with illustrations, can overcome the problem. Split interviewing also makes possible the use of more complex scalar questions than is feasible over the phone.

The extension of telephone interviewing is therefore very flexible and can be adapted to many situations where otherwise expensive personal visits would be required.

THE FIRST PART OF THE SPLIT INTERVIEW

Two areas are pursued in the first part of the split interview:

1. Obtaining information which is not dependent on the mailed material.
2. Seeking further cooperation.

The information in the first part of the split interview covers current behaviour and perhaps attitudes to established products. Information may also be obtained to filter out respondents who do not justify the follow-up interview, perhaps because they do not use sufficient volumes of a product.

The request for further cooperation is made towards the end of this first interview and up to this point the approach is exactly the same as for any other telephone interview. Only at the end of this first contact and when all the questions have been asked, is the request made for further cooperation. By this point the interviewer and the respondent will have created a rapport and a relationship, and any concerns about being able to answer the questions will have been dispelled. Having helped to this point, few respondents refuse to cooperate with the follow on part. A useful approach is to use the information already given as a basis for the next stage:

I really am very interested in what you have told me Mr xxx. Because of your experience I would like to take this one step further and mail you some information about the new product. I am sure you will find it very interesting. I could then phone you back and see what you think of it.

Because cooperation in this type of research is usually good, incentives tend not to be necessary. There are exceptions, for example, when the respondent is asked to undertake a time-consuming exercise or where, by custom, the respondent group has come to expect payment (this applies to the medical field, for example). Also, while a real incentive may not be necessary, some nominal token may be worth considering — such as a novelty pen.

The telephone questionnaire used for the first stage of the split interview should have space to record when the mailing was sent to the respondent and any notes to help the interviewer at the time of the follow up.

THE MAILOUT STAGE OF THE SPLIT INTERVIEW

Care is needed in the design of the mailout material. Though a very high standard of presentation is not essential, the material should nevertheless be clear and look professional.

Any written text should be kept short and a single page is ideal as anything longer probably won't be read. Written descriptions should be clear and jargon avoided unless it is reasonably certain that the terms will be understood by the respondents (if mailing readers of computer magazines, for example, some 'computerese' is acceptable). Mailouts to domestic customers should avoid all jargon and use short, simple words.

In new product market research, a balance has to be kept between providing full data on the product and overselling it. Although less obvious features and benefits may have to be stated, superlatives and puffery should be avoided.

The written material can be reproduced from a type-written original provided the printer and copier are of a decent standard.

Often a visual is included with the mailout. This can be a photograph, an illustration from a printed source, or a drawing. If only a fairly short run is required (up to 100 or so) photographs can be reproduced photographically at a modest cost. Some photographic suppliers can print on thin paper. However, many amateur photographs are technically unacceptable and it may be necessary to commission professional help.

Sales literature for a product is often unsuitable as a mailout as it is designed to sell the product rather than act as a research tool. However, illustrations or perhaps data tables culled from the brochures are often usable if they are supported by the researcher's own text.

A drawing is often a better form of visual than a photograph as features and functions can be conveyed much more clearly. Also, in new product research the design may not have gone beyond the concept stage and only a drawing is possible. Assistance is likely to be needed in preparing the drawing. Brief the illustrator well and describe exactly what is required and how the finished illustration should look. Generally, a simple perspective drawing, rather than a plan, is what is required.

A covering letter must accompany the mailing. This should remind the respondent of the research, describe what action is required and indicate if and when any further contact will be made by the interviewer.

Make sure that the mailout is adequately packed: this applies particularly when sample products are mailed.

FOLLOW-UP WITHIN THE SPLIT INTERVIEW

Allow between three and five days before re-contacting the respondent. If the respondent is expected to try out a product, a longer wait may be needed.

Cooperation in follow-up interviews is nearly always good. Having been interviewed initially and agreed to participate further, few respondents refuse at the follow-up stage. Interviewers do not need to waste time and money getting through to the right person since they have already been identified. For this reason, the cost of each follow-up interview is low in relation to the initial interviews. However, 'wastage' of 10 to 20 per cent must be anticipated, perhaps because the mailout fails to reach the respondent, or he doesn't get round to doing what has been asked, or is just never available on re-contact.

The follow-up interview itself is much like any other administered by telephone although the preliminaries can be largely dispensed with. The follow-up is therefore very efficient as nearly all the phone time is spent obtaining information.

The mailout itself does not necessarily include questions if there is a follow-up by phone. However, scalar questions can be included with the mailout and the responses can be collected verbally during the phone re-contact. It should be made clear in the covering letter, however, that this is to be the procedure.

9

DEPTH INTERVIEWING TECHNIQUES

■

Sometimes the term 'depth' or 'in-depth' is bandied around by market researchers without a precise meaning. There is an implication that the depth interview is face-to-face, a suggestion that it is longer rather than shorter and that being unstructured, it allows the respondent to dig deep, talk freely and so uncover true motivations. Very often the interview is tape recorded rather than written down on a questionnaire. Depth interviews stand alongside group discussions at the heart of qualitative research.

Some people are natural interviewers. They make you want to tell them everything. Perhaps some of the aptitude of interviewing is a gift but much can be learned. This chapter looks at ways in which interviewers can improve their technique in depth interviews.

THE ROOTS OF INTERVIEWING

LISTENING v TALKING

There is nobody more interesting than someone who is interested in you; genuinely interested in you. The natural interviewers are those who have a curiosity about other people, who are more interested in others than they are in themselves, who are listeners rather than talkers.

Listening carefully to a respondent is imperative in good interviewing. First and foremost, listening indicates to the respondent that the interviewer is *interested* and there can be no finer compliment to what someone is saying. Furthermore, listening to and understanding what is being said is necessary to facilitate the deeper lines of questioning which are the substance of depth interviewing.

Working out the right ratio of talking to listening is a personal thing and could vary, depending on the subject and the conditions. The very act of asking questions takes time. So too it may be that some of the interviewer's talk could be aimed at relaxing the respondent, perhaps sharing some feelings or providing asides which bring the interview nearer to a conversation and further away from an interrogation. As a generalisation the interviewer should expect to occupy no more than 10 to 20 per cent of the tape transcription with the greater input from the respondent.

BUILDING RAPPORT

Successful interviewers have an easy style which helps respondents relax and feel confident. This build up of understanding makes a respondent want to tell all. Understanding is a two-way process which comes from sharing feelings, knowledge and experiences and therefore demands an input from the interviewer. It is during this first stage of the interview that the interviewer will be aiming to build rapport and get 'on the same wavelength'.

REDUCING TENSION

Tension in an interview is caused by worries on the part of the respondent. Why me? Will I be able to answer the questions? Will I make a fool of myself? Why is this being taped? Will it get me into trouble? How long is this going to go on for? What is *really* going on?

Many of the feelings arise out of not knowing what is in store, perhaps fearing that the interview will be more difficult or taxing than it really is. As the questions unfold and the respondent gets into a stride, confidence builds and tension falls. The questioning process itself acts to reduce tension as long as the early questions are well within the respondent's competence.

In the face-to-face situation which is typical of depth interviews, it is usual for the interviewer to spend a short time on pleasantries to make the respondent feel easy. Of course, sympathy must be shown for the circumstances as it would increase the tension if an interviewer spent five minutes on the 'warm up' when the respondent was very obviously pushed for time and eager to press on.

The figure below shows how levels of tension vary during an interview with a peak in stress levels as the interview gets under way and a relaxation as the rapport builds and confidence is gained.

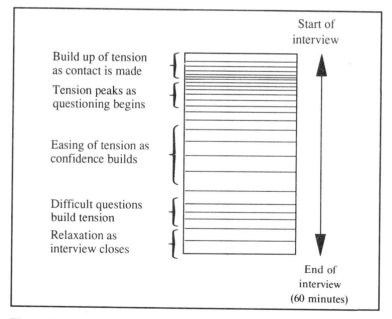

Figure 9.1 Levels of tension in a depth interview

If time allows it can be helpful for the interviewer to spend the first minute or so putting the study in some form of context. People like to know 'what it is all about' as a study without an apparent purpose is unsettling. This need not mean disclosing the whole and underlying purpose of the study but it should be enough to make the respondent feel that the time spent at his or her expense will not be wasted.

Interviewing is very much a matter of style and the techniques adopted by one person may not work for another. So, for example, some interviewers may use 'self disclosure' as a device to let the respondent know that they have similar feelings and to create a bond. So, too, humour can be successful in reducing tension. However, badly handled self disclosure could come across as patronising while a joke which falls flat is most certainly worse than no joke at all.

During the interview it is best to adopt a business-like approach assuming a show of quiet confidence and an aura of control. The respondent will settle down, happy to be in the hands of a competent interviewer and looking forward to things happening smoothly and efficiently. In setting the scene it could be appropriate to run briefly through the agenda explaining what will happen and how long it will all take.

CREATING INTEREST

Enthusiasm is contagious and will help win cooperation. After the third group discussion of the day or the fifth depth interview, the interviewer may well be feeling jaded but for the respondent this is not routine and it may be a considerable time since they were last interviewed. Above all else, people are interested in themselves. Since the whole of the interview is an opportunity for the respondent to talk about what he or she does and thinks, this gives the interviewer a considerable advantage. Moving the discussion on to the respondent is a sure way of building interest. The first question should be one to get the respondent talking and it could provide some framework for understanding the replies: 'Tell me about the work you do here? What does it involve?'

People are also interested in things which are new. If one of the angles of the research is to find out what people want so that products can be modified or developed to meet those needs, then this could be exploited: 'The research will help the development of new products and I will be asking what you think about some new concepts.'

USING BODY LANGUAGE AS A CLUE TO RESPONSES

People's body language can provide clues as to whether what they are saying is what they are thinking. These postures also provide indicators which show if a respondent is telling the truth or if they are bottled up and tense. The experienced interviewer watches for this non-verbal leakage and uses it to interpret what is said or to relax the respondent if they seem uptight.

Sometimes body language is all too obvious. A rapid tattoo on the desk with the fingers is a clear sign of impatience, and it does not require an expert to interpret a yawn or drooping eyelids.

Over the years we have learned to control our actions so that much of what we feel is not evident by how we look or our voice when we speak. We are, therefore, looking for very small clues and using them as just one input in the interpretation.

Body language sends out clues which show if the respondent is relaxed or tense. People feel safer behind some form of physical blockade and so a desk or table can provide a shield. Take away the businessman's desk, remove him from his day-to-day environment and place him in a hotel for a group discussion and the defences fall. When a respondent is taken from his or her comfort zone they seek protection by crossing their arms or hands in front of their body. And out of the security of their own environment they are far more vulnerable to probing questions than behind the protection of a three-foot-wide desk.

In a one-to-one interview, personal space assumes considerable importance. We are conditioned to require an acceptable margin of space between ourselves and strangers and the interviewer, as a stranger, could become threatening unless distanced by at least three or four feet. If seated, both respondent and interviewer will feel easier if situated at right angles to each other, so removing the confrontational position of sitting face-to-face.

As the interview progresses the respondent could display any one of a number of physical signals. Figure 9.2 illustrates seven types of signals on a *believability* scale which indicates the extent to which the respondent could be lying.

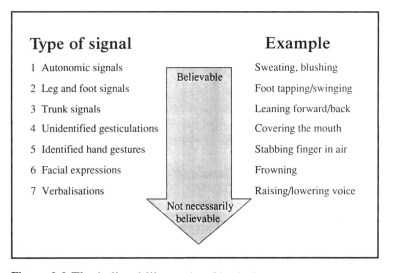

Figure 9.2 The believability scale of body language

1.   *Autonomic signals.* These are actions which are beyond our deliberate control and indicate how we are really feeling. They include sweating, blushing or going pale. It is impossible to sweat at will or to quicken the breathing. These things happen under stress and indicate to the interviewer that there is embarrassment, tension or something amiss.

2.   *Leg and foot signals.* The legs and feet are a part of the body which people do not control, believing them to be out of sight and mind. The desk can be a barrier to what is happening in the nether regions during an interview and it is one reason why businessmen prefer to give an interview partially hidden behind it. Non-verbal leakage may exist as

the respondent kicks his feet or wraps feet and legs closely together in an attempt to gain comfort or hide the truth.

3.   *Trunk signals.* In some circumstances a respondent may wish to hide his or her true feelings but fails to do so because their body language gives the game away. The body tells us if the respondent is attentive and interested or bored and tired. Someone sitting upright and towards the edge of their chair appears to be (and probably is) more responsive and alert than someone slumped in their seat with their head back. However, the latter may be more receptive to that difficult question, perhaps being off guard.

4.   *Unidentified gesticulations.* In situations where people are known to be lying, it is more likely that they will have a higher than average hand-to-head action. During periods of deception the 'nose touch' and 'mouth cover' are the most typical of the gestures. Covering the mouth when saying something which is not true arises from a sub-conscious desire to gag the false words which are emerging. When people touch their nose, fan their fingers over their mouth, rest their forefinger on their upper lip or have their hand at the side of their mouth, it does not necessarily mean they are lying, it simply means that lying is a possibility and may indicate that the respondent is unsure about the data or that information is being held back.

5.   *Identified hand gestures.* Sometimes respondents make very precise hand gestures, stabbing the air or hitting the desk for emphasis. For most people these are managed reactions and cannot be assumed to say much about the respondent except that they are under control.

6.   *Facial expressions.* We are so aware of our faces that it is easy for us to lie with them. Even here there can be some clues depending on the skill and experience of the respondent. The eyes especially can be revealing. They may shift to the side when someone is unsure of an answer. They could look away or narrow. There could be inadvertent puckering of the brow or tightening of the jaw muscles; momentary lapses that tell us something is not as it should be. The big smile or the deep frown may hide natural feelings and they may also alert us to be on the look-out.

7. *Verbalisations.* Finally, what people say is not what they necessarily mean. It is for this reason that it is last on the believability scale, and is why we need to be aware of body language and in particular to turn to projective techniques which allow us to search beyond the obvious and the overt.

PROJECTIVE INTERVIEWING TECHNIQUES

REASONS FOR USING PROJECTIVE INTERVIEWING TECHNIQUES

Projective interviewing techniques are used in qualitative research to overcome the barriers of communication between the informant and the interviewer. These barriers exist for a number of reasons.

■ Embarrassment can prevent a respondent admitting to behaviour which is viewed as socially unacceptable. Take, for example, circumstances when our behaviour is in-admissible to others. Most people at some time or another have been susceptible to dalliances such as the avoidance of tube fares, pocketing excess change given to them in error, taking pens home from the office, having the odd drink too many and driving. But these are things we would prefer to forget and not admit in an interview.

■ Beyond the embarrassing questions there are those which are sensitive, verging on the inviolate. Social, cultural or behavioural constraints may influence the answers. Take, for example, an in-home interview which asks about personal hygiene and the use of deodorant. A respondent whose bathing habits are rather relaxed may exaggerate the frequency of washing and the use of deodorant to avoid a sense of shame in front of the interviewer. Sensitive subjects are likely to include hygiene, sex, money, status, health, death and education. In businesses respondents may be reticent to discuss prices, margins, purchase volumes, sources of purchases, investment intentions and new product developments.

- Sometimes respondents want to please the interviewer and give an answer that they think is appropriate to the survey. This can happen in readership surveys where the respondent, inclined to the view that there is some kudos to be gained from reading a wide range of papers or journals, exaggerates the numbers and frequency with which they are read.
- People assume that they alone act rationally. It is commonplace to hear respondents say that they are not influenced by advertising, that they buy a car because it is safe and comfortable and that they choose a brand of beer for its taste. However, the same people, if asked why their neighbours have bought a certain car, believe that they were gullible enough to be influenced by its style and performance. Advertising works for other people but we, the rational consumers, are above its Machiavellian persuasion. Others may buy a car for its style and performance but we would not be so garish. Whereas others cannot tell the subtle difference between Boddingtons and Tetleys, we are far more discriminating. Uncovering the motivations in buying behaviour is the job of depth interviewing and projective techniques can be a considerable help.
- For some people it is difficult to find the right words to answer a question. They may not be able to articulate their emotions, indeed they may not even know what they are. People say that they like going to the cinema for the big screen but could it be that they also crave being in the company of others? They say that they need a large car for the ride quality but could it be a power symbol? They say that they need to run six miles a day to keep fit but could they be running away from something?

Direct questioning on any of these issues could draw a blank or invoke an answer which is thought to be acceptable, perhaps even given in ignorance and believed to be correct. Worse, direct questioning on some of the sensitive subjects could create a barrier which mars subsequent cooperation. In such circumstances, projective interviewing techniques are used.

PROJECTIVE TECHNIQUES WHICH USE WORDS TO GET PEOPLE THINKING ABOUT A SUBJECT

Indirect question

The indirect question is probably the most common of all the projective interviewing techniques. The interviewer asks a question about what other people think or do and so removes the subject from the respondent. For example, in business-to-business interviews it can be difficult to get people to talk about the prices they are paying for products. The indirect question would be:

Thinking about . . . (STATE TYPE OF PRODUCT), what would be a typical price paid by someone in this industry who was buying about 10,000 units per year?

The price which the respondent gives may not be precisely that which the respondent pays himself but, by speaking the words, the taboo has been broken and the interviewer can gauge the mood of the situation. It could easily lead on to further questions:

And from your own company's point of view, would the price you pay be higher or lower than this figure?

Instead of asking outright, 'How much do you pay for X?', the indirect approach creeps up on the subject so that the respondent gives away bits at a time until all may as well be revealed.

This approach is sometimes called the *Third person test* as respondents are asked to describe what other people (the third persons) would do in certain circumstances.

Word association/sentence completion/story completion

A very simple projective technique is to ask respondents to think of words which are associated with a product or brand. Equally, the questions could focus on a product and the respondents are asked what feelings or words come to mind. In a group discussion about hot drinks of various kinds, the words coffee, tea and hot chocolate produced the following array of words. Just looking through them gives a feel for the positioning of the drinks and their strengths and weaknesses.

Coffee	Tea	Hot Chocolate
Perky	Afternoon	Bedtime
Morning	Refreshing	Winter
Aroma	Morning	Family
Black	Weak	Story time
Strong	Cheap	Sweet
Filter	Ladies	Children
Palpitations	Biscuits	Friendly

Sentence completion is a development of word association. The interviewer reads out or shows the beginnings of sentences and asks the respondent to add an ending. As with word association, this is done at rapid tempo to ensure that instantaneous replies are obtained and that the answers are spontaneous rather than too considered.

The sentences can vary from being open in format to those which are more focused and constrain the replies. It can be useful to have both types in a battery, for example:

If only there was a hot drink which . . .
When I have a cup of tea I think . . .
The nicest thing about coffee is . . .

PROJECTIVE TECHNIQUES WHICH EXTEND PEOPLE'S IMAGINATIONS LATERALLY

Analogy/symbolic analogy

Thinking about a subject in another context can be a means of opening up the mind. Respondents may be asked to think of a brand as a person or an object:

If the car was a person, what sort of person would it be?

The resulting answers may give many clues as to the views on the car. Is the nominated person male or female? Young or old? Classy, stylish or boring? What would the car do for a living? Where would the car go on holiday? What type of books would the car read? Through the conversion of an object to a person the personality of the object could be made clearer.

As an example, a study was carried out into people's perceptions of organisations which carry out market research. These included market research companies, management consultancies and academic institutions. A large number of respondents in the study suggested that the consultancies were typified by one or other of the 'big cat family' implying such organisations were powerful, fast, perhaps even predatory. The academic institutions were positioned as owls and elephants; the one clever, the other with a long memory though also characterised by being large and slow. Market research companies, on the other hand, had no distinct image as an animal of any kind, suggesting that they lacked a strong identity.

This type of questioning could be developed so that a brand or product is considered in abstract terms on the grounds that it can be more difficult to 'make up' a reply that reflects feelings rather than one which has to be explained:

'What colour or colours come to mind when you think of . . .?'
'What music comes to mind when you think of . . .?'

Fantasy

In this type of questioning, respondents are asked to imagine a fantasy world, perhaps one where the start of the fantasy has been mapped out for them by the interviewer. They then take over, involving the product or brand in some way or another. Getting people to think in fantasies is one way of encouraging them to think laterally about a subject, removing the shackles of normal thinking, and so opening up a discussion about a product in different ways and perhaps uncovering hidden angles. The subject need not be a weird fantasy; it could be a simple story which the respondent has to complete.

Future scenario

As the title of this device suggests, the respondent is asked to describe the future, including the position and role of the product at that time. The way it fits in to society, the uses to which it is put, the modifications to the product itself, may all give clues as to its strengths and weaknesses.

Obituary

Respondents may be asked to write an obituary for a product, bringing out its good and bad points and saying why it eventually disappeared.

PROJECTIVE TECHNIQUES INVOLVING DRAWINGS OR MAKING THINGS IN ORDER TO DEVELOP PEOPLE'S VIEWS ON A SUBJECT

Cartoons

In this method of questioning the respondent is faced with a picture depicting a situation. The situation is deliberately vague, with balloons rising out of the characters ready to contain their words or thoughts. One of the balloons may be left blank for the respondent to fill in. Through the interpretation of the drawing, the respondent is projecting his or her own thoughts but doing so into a neutral environment (the picture).

The technique works well in both consumer and business-to-business interviews and is particularly suited to situations where the answers are not so obvious and need a little thought. In the following example, the subject of research was buyers of engineering components. The cartoon presented a number of different sales arguments from suppliers of components and respondents were asked to state which of the thought bubbles was most appropriate.

SITUATION 1   SITUATION 2

SITUATION 1

I wonder if they are? And, if they are, I wonder how long he can keep it up. Still, it could be worth a try.

Just give me a chance. Our prices are as keen as you will find anywhere.

SITUATION 2

Do I really want to pay a premium for quality?

We only stock quality products. We are BS 5750 registered. You may pay a bit more from us but the quality of the goods and the service will never let you down.

Figure 9.3 Example of balloon drawing

The cartoon tests flush out the *hidden* feelings and thoughts and are not a substitute for open-ended questioning.

An extension of the cartoon drawings is the *Thematic Apperception Test*. This technique has been borrowed from clinical psychology and comprises deliberately indistinct and ambiguous drawings, the subject of which is not obvious at all. For the most part these are human figures in situations which the respondents have to describe and, in so doing, uncover their own thoughts and prejudices. This is the type of technique which every marketing student learns about but it is seldom used in its pure sense in every day market research.

Ink blot test

The Rorschach ink blot test is another socio-psychological device for finding out people's hidden feelings but in twenty years in market research I have never seen it used. It is another subject for the text books and exam papers. The theory behind the test is that haphazard shapes, in the first instance created by ink blots, were given to respondents to examine and decipher.

This test may be useful to psychologists in exploring Freudian hang-ups but it is doubtful that it explains much about consumer behaviour in the marketplace.

Picture association/interpretation

It is quite common in groups to show respondents a board on which there are many pictures of houses or people. The respondents are then asked to link the product under discussion with one of the pictures in an attempt to 'position' it more closely. For example:

> 'If the product was to live in any one of the houses shown on this board, which would it be?'
> 'And if the product was a person, which of the people shown on this board would it be?'

(See Figure 9.4 overleaf.)

Psychodrawing

Respondents are given drawing materials and asked to create a picture which represents their view of a product or brand. The final drawing may show aspects which are hard to put into words. Moreover, the drawing may become a discussion point which allows the respondent to explain their thinking at the time and it is this which provides the insights. The subject and the respondents have to be right to achieve a successful result with psychodrawing. Respondents should be creative though not necessarily good artists as their artistic representation means far less than the colours and general theme of the drawing.

Modelling

For completeness in this section it is necessary to mention modelling as a means of finding out what people think. This is another of the techniques often quoted in text books but which are seldom, if ever, used. Theoretically, people are given plasticine or modelling clay and asked to make a representation of the product or subject under study. These approaches fall down because they are heavily dependent on some level of modelling skill and the respondent's mind is on how to make an acceptable shape rather than communicating a subtle feeling.

PROJECTIVE TECHNIQUES WHICH INVOLVE PEOPLE IN ROLE PLAYING

Psychodrama

In this projective technique respondents are asked to role play, acting parts which have been ascribed to them by the moderator. For example, one person may be asked to play the role of a salesman and the other the role of a buyer. Positioning people in conflicting situations can be a powerful means of flushing out arguments as each defends their position. Interesting results can be achieved by asking people who do not hold a particular view to argue its case in order to find out if and how this changes their opinion on the subject.

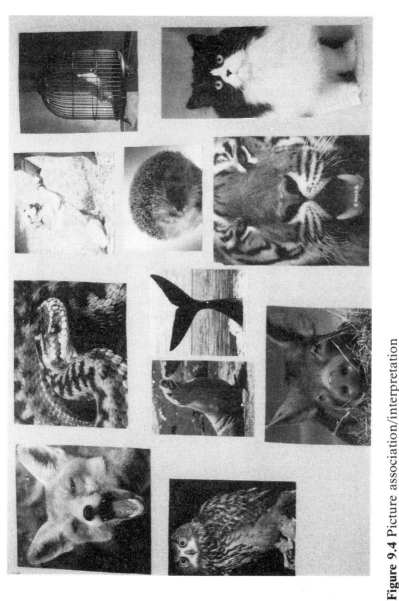

Figure 9.4 Picture association/interpretation

These are two examples of storyboards. The top board shows a variety of people representing different lifestyles; the bottom one shows animals which respondents would be asked to associate with products.

This type of research can only work if the respondents are sufficiently creative and of the right frame of mind. Role playing may be considered appropriate for an extended group and it could be something that the interviewer tries if the group has gelled and a good rapport has developed. Without this spark, role playing would fall flat.

FINDING SUITABLE CANDIDATES FOR PROJECTIVE INTERVIEWING TECHNIQUES

Getting people to be creative and asking them to open up their minds is not always easy. Sometimes projective techniques fail because respondents cannot see the relevance or are unable to think of a reply. When 700 owners of Honda Civics were asked to imagine that their car was an animal and to suggest what that would be, only a half could do so.

Since group discussions are very often the occasion when the more imaginative of the enabling techniques are attempted, it is wise to think about screening questions to ensure that only creative people attend. The screening questions for recruitment to the groups could include some sentence completion or symbolic analogy tests or they could verge on the wacky. For example:

'Think of as many uses as possible for a house brick.'

10

OVERCOMING OBJECTIONS

THE PROBLEM OF LOW COOPERATION RATES

There is a paucity of firm data to show the level of respondent cooperation in market research surveys. These figures are easier to keep track of in telephone surveys where the interviewers record on contact sheets the reasons for failing to achieve the interview. Typically cooperation rates are 60 to 70 per cent in both consumer and business-to-business telephone surveys. The proportion is likely to be lower if the subject is touchy such as finance (sensitive) or home improvements (closely allied with selling) and would be higher if it related to something of interest and relevance (eg about a recent car purchase).

In business-to-business surveys there is a wide variability in levels of cooperation depending on the subject and type of respondent. However, the cooperation rate is nearly always lower in the case of face-to-face interviews than for telephone interviews. This is because respondents are, by and large, prepared to give up ten minutes of their time to help 'on the spot' in a short telephone interview but they need extra persuasion to find an hour (or will it be two hours?) in their busy diaries. Buyers for the large retailing groups are notoriously hard to interview while people buying or specifying machine tools are not overtaxed by market researchers and are much more inclined to talk.

Cooperation rates in consumer household and street interviewing are much more difficult to ascertain as the rejection rate is not usually a required measurement. In the main, interviewers have to achieve a quota of respondents and are not obliged to record how many refused, fell outside the quota or took avoiding action by not answering the door or walking on the other side of the street. Received wisdom is that cooperation rates are around the 50 per cent mark and not a lot more. This raises serious concerns about the 'ones that get away' as their exclusion from the survey could bias the results if they are atypical in some way. There is an obvious need to achieve as high cooperation rates as possible in all types of survey and this is the subject of this chapter.

UNDERSTANDING THE REASONS FOR OBJECTIONS

Objections to taking part in a market research survey can be anti-cipated in any interview programme. Dealing with them is rather like a game of tennis. The respondent voices an objection which is analogous to sending a good ball on to your side of the net. It is up to you to deal with that ball and return it. Your rejoinder may be sufficiently good to win you the point and the interview can begin. Alternatively, the respondent could either return the same ball or decide to serve another. The task of the interviewer is to keep batting the ball across to the other side of the net until it stays there, at which time the interview can start.

WINNING COOPERATION

The best approach to successful interviewing is to avoid situations which raise objections by *making the respondent want to help* from the outset.

LEGITIMACY

Most people want to help others — if they believe that they need help. To take an example outside market research, a charity which seeks funds for a cataclysmic act of God will receive more donations than one where it is felt that the victims somehow shouldn't have been there in the first place or who perhaps brought the tragedy upon themselves. So too, fund-raising for a disaster close to home will win more support than will one for a larger catastrophe which is far away.

Turning the discussion back to market research, people similarly have got to identify with a survey and believe that their contribution will help if they are to see it as legitimate and worthwhile.

Now the legitimacy of the survey, just like that of the charity, is all the more powerful if it is identifiable. Collecting money to buy more books and to raise educational standards across the country has less pulling power than a request to help a named, local school. Extending this analogy into the market research situation it can be seen that the interviewer will achieve more success if he or she presents the case on a personal level rather than on a group level. For example:

> 'I wonder if you would be kind enough to help me. My name is Paul Hague and I am carrying out a project on . . . and would appreciate it if you could spare a few minutes of your time' (etc).

is likely to be more successful than:

> 'I work for Business & Market Research who is carrying out a survey about . . .; it will only take a few minutes of your time' (etc).

In the first instance the stronger personalisation of the request would encourage the instinct to help, whereas in the latter example the obligation to help has been masked by introducing the name of a company. Of course, the name of the research sponsor or the name of the company must be mentioned at some time during the introduction for otherwise the respondent could be misled into thinking that the survey was a private project and not one destined for a wider audience. However, the declaration of the sponsors could be unfolded as the respondent becomes committed to helping.

'. . . Thank you for agreeing to help; I do appreciate it. Let me assure you that this is a bona fide market research survey and your replies will be confidential and used as part of a wider analysis. I work for Business & Market Research plc who are bound by the rules of the Market Research Society and to whose standards we conform.'

A survey gains legitimacy if people can see a relationship between themselves and the research sponsor. In a survey carried out with buyers of Honda cars it made sense to explain why respondents had been singled out and contacted.

'The survey is being carried out for Honda who value the views of their customers.'

The agonies over the legitimacy of market research do not rest entirely with respondents; interviewers too may have doubts as to why the study is being carried out. These misgivings could influence their approach on the doorstep or on the phone. If the interviewer lacks conviction, the manner of the approach will be poor, the respondent will sense the weakness and the interview could be lost.

BENEFITS AND COSTS

In most market research interviews respondents do not receive payment for their trouble. Even when they do (as is the case in group discussions or in interviews with doctors) it is generally a modest sum, becoming more substantial where it is believed that the only way of winning cooperation is to pay handsomely for the respondents' time and trouble. Once a respondent believes that the survey is legitimate and relevant, he or she will decide if they are interested enough to help.

There is a certain level of intrinsic interest in some subjects and this can vary according to circumstances. The more important a subject is in someone's life, the more interesting it is sure to be. Thus an interview about a recent car purchase is more interesting than one about writing paper. In an industrial situation the buyer will be more interested in the bigger items in the company's shopping basket than in those which are incidental.

However, interest can be created. The enthusiasm of the interviewer is an important contributor to generating regard for the survey. Similarly, interest in the interviewer can be enough to engage people's help. An experiment I observed convinced me that a smartly dressed interviewer has more success in winning cooperation in street interviews than one who is dowdy. In the same way, a pleasant voice over the telephone will have its own attraction and become an interest factor which builds the cooperation rate.

Going beyond the interest in the subject and the interviewer, it is possible to generate interest in the process of research itself. This proposition could appeal to the practical respondents who want to know how something works. They may appreciate some explanation about who else is being interviewed, how many people are in the sample and where the names came from.

Yet another group of respondents may genuinely welcome the chance to talk to someone about what they think and believe. Undoubtedly some of these will be people on an ego trip while others may simply be lonely.

BELIEF IN THE ABILITY TO HELP

People have a fear of making fools of themselves. They do not want to place themselves in a position where they cannot answer questions or where they voluntarily invite the stress of examination. Since respondents are unaware of the questions which will be asked, they will assume the worst. As a result, they may be inclined to make an excuse, to refuse to help or attempt to redirect the interviewer to someone for whom the survey is more apposite. The interviewer must recognise these fears, check them out and appease the prospective interviewee.

PERSONAL RESPONSIBILITY

Thinking again about the analogy of winning support for charities, we know that there is often a feeling that our help won't be missed. And even if we were to help, the effect would be so minimal as to be irrelevant. It does not take much to justify doing nothing. Respondents need reassurance that their help *is* important and that what they are being asked to do will be well within their capability.

The consideration that market research is someone else's problem arises out of a lack of personal responsibility. Respondents should be made to believe that they have a real contribution to make and that the survey will suffer without them. This may be especially so in industrial surveys where there are few companies in the market and every one counts.

> 'I really do need your help to meet my quota of interviews today. Finding people who are eligible for the survey can be difficult and I know what problems it will create for me if you say no.'

Or

> 'The survey is based on a carefully controlled sampling method and so it is very important to me that everyone who is contacted actually helps. It makes the results much more reliable. If you don't mind trying a few questions we could see how we get on . . .'

CONFIDENCE AS A MEANS OF WINNING COOPERATION

The starting point for winning cooperation at interviews is the right attitude. The best interviewers are confident people. The confidence they have in themselves gives them charge of the situation and transmits to the respondents who are happy to be in their capable hands. The converse is also true. A diffident or insecure interviewer will make the respondent feel uneasy and they will be more likely to refuse cooperation.

Associated with confidence, enthusiasm also wins cooperation. Enthusiasm is contagious and makes the respondent want to take part.

Below are some examples of openers from taped interviews with successful interviewers. They are taken from a survey carried out over the telephone with people who use and specify franking machines.

Interviewer: 'Could you put me through to your mail room manager please.'

Receptionist: 'I am sorry we don't have a mail room manager here.'

Interviewer: 'I'll try your office manager then.'

Receptionist: 'Actually, we don't have an office manager as such either.'

Interviewer: 'Well I wonder if you could help me. I am trying to get hold of the person who would decide on the type of franking machine you use. Who would that be?'

Receptionist: 'Well the person who would actually buy it is Mr Jackson, but he doesn't see anyone. The franking is done by Joan Kinvig but she is out until later this afternoon.'

Interviewer: 'Thank you for that advice. Would you mind telling me what time I could best catch Miss Kinvig?'

Receptionist: 'Try sometime after 3.'

Interviewer: 'Thank you I will. By the way, just for my records, can I ask your name.'

Receptionist: 'It is Val Bryning.'

Later that afternoon the interviewer called back.

Interviewer: 'Hello again. This is Janice Longman here. I called earlier today about a franking machine survey I am carrying out. Is Joan Kinvig in yet?'

Receptionist: 'I'll put you through.'

Interviewer: 'Hello. My name is Janice Longman. I called earlier today and was talking to Val Bryning who said that you would be the best person to talk to me about franking machines. I am trying to find out what people who use franking machines think of them. Can I ask what model you use at . . .'

And the interview began. The interviewer had worked out a strategy before contacting the company and was able to move between asking for a person with a certain position to finding out who best fitted the position even though there was no one with exactly that title. The opportunity was passed over to interview Mr Jackson because he was not identified as a hands-on user and it could have blocked further contact with the company. The option was seized to interview the person who used the machine and the opportunity was taken to give the survey some legitimacy by mentioning a colleague's name by way of introduction. Finally, the interviewer kept the introduction short and led straight in with the first question.

The next example is from the same survey but here the interviewer meets an objection that becomes insuperable.

Interviewer:	'Good morning. Could you put me through to your mail room manager.'
Receptionist:	'We don't have a mail room manager as such. Could one of the secretaries who organises the post help?'
Secretary:	'Hello.'
Interviewer:	'Good morning. This is Veronica Ashton from Business & Market Research in Stockport. We are carrying out a survey of people's attitudes to their franking machines. Could I ask if you are the person who would buy a new machine?'
Secretary:	'No, it would be our finance director.'
Interviewer:	'Do you think I could speak to him?'
Secretary:	'He's tied up right now.'
Interviewer:	'Could I call back at a more convenient time?'
Secretary:	'I really should tell you that I don't think we are interested.'
Interviewer:	'The questions are really quite simple, they won't take long, I promise.'
Secretary:	'No, I'm sorry I have to go now. I'm sorry we can't help.'

Things began to go wrong for this interviewer when she asked the secretary if she was the person who would buy a new machine. It would have been better to have opened a conversation with the secretary to find out what role she played in the company's use of franking machines since it is possible she could have become an ally in winning the interview. Certainly, she would have been able to fill in some background on the company's use of franking machines and, as a result, the interviewer would have learned something and developed a rapport which may have led to cooperation. Once the secretary started to become negative, it became easier with every subsequent question to say no until eventually, there was no problem freezing the interviewer out.

Sometimes it is better to be indirect with questioning as a direct question could elicit the answer no from which it is difficult to recover. Thus, as an alternative to asking 'Do you think I could speak to him?' it may be better to find out more about what is going on by saying 'Just so that I understand things more fully, could you explain to me what role your Finance Director plays in buying franking machines?' Questions which require an explanation for an answer are less likely to be refused and more likely to generate useful information.

The interviewer treads a fine line between persistence and browbeating the respondent. This is partly because interviewers know that most interviews need 'selling in' and, when success is finally achieved, respondents actually quite enjoy the process.

SOME GUIDELINES TO WINNING COOPERATION

To gain the interview the researcher needs qualities of salesmanship. Interviewers have no product or service to sell, only their personalities and the intangible possibility of improvements to future products and services. In the interviewer's favour, most people have a high level of interest in themselves and interviewing brings the focus right down on this subject. To be singled out to talk about what they do and think and be under no pressure to buy is an indulgence and ego boost.

The interviewer is working towards the overriding goal of obtaining the cooperation of the person who should be interviewed. It is important that the interviewer has worked out an introduction before attempting contact. A fluent, bright and breezy approach is needed. An apologetic or reticent approach invites rejection.

Here are a number of tips to bear in mind in formulating a successful introduction:

1. *Where possible, mention a mutual contact:* If a third party can be named as the person who suggested the contact, the respondent will feel involved, possibly obligated. In a business-to-business interview this approach could work as follows: 'John Davis, marketing director of Davis & Clark mentioned your name and said that you would be likely to help me in a survey I am carrying out into precision ground bar', or 'I have just been speaking to your project engineer, Terry Knowles, about solenoid valves. He suggested that if I telephone you, you may be able to help with a survey I am carrying out'.

2. *Be brief:* Long-winded explanations may exasperate and alienate the respondent. However, where necessary, be prepared to develop a rapport to gain confidence.

3. *Justify the visit* by suggesting a benefit to the respondent (a newer, better product, improved service, etc).

4. *Appease the respondent's conscience and concern:* Some respondents cannot imagine that they know enough to help. If the interviewer says that he or she will be visiting another firm in the area at the same time, a would-be respondent may feel happier agreeing to the meeting believing that the pressure to provide 'all the answers' is relieved because there is another respondent who will be carrying some of the responsibility for making the trip worthwhile.

5. *Suggest a time and date that suits you* — but be ready with an alternative. Be prepared to call back.

6. *Give assurances:* If you know the respondent is the right person but claims not to know enough to be able to help, give an assurance that the interview does not demand right or wrong answers as it is opinions that count. If facts are required, say that estimates are acceptable. Always be prepared to give a reference in the form of a letter from the company or an interviewer's identity card. Where

OVERCOMING OBJECTIONS ■ 101

confidentiality is posed as a problem, give assurances, in
writing if necessary.

7. *Confirm the arrangements by letter:* When an interview is set
up with a company, it is best to confirm the arrangements
by letter, restating the purpose of the visit, confirming the
time and venue and thanking the respondent in anticipation.
This reduces the possibility of misunderstandings and provides the respondent with some 'official' statement of who
is doing the work.

Unfortunately, life is never simple and problems will arise.
Sometimes these are peculiar to the survey or the company, and
native wit must be used in overcoming them. Nevertheless there
are some common problems which can more easily be countered
if prior thought has been given. Some frequently occurring problems and pitfalls are discussed below.

■ **Never accept as definite a meeting that has been arranged by
someone else.** You may, for example, speak to a colleague
in the same office who says he is sure the respondent will
help if you call on a certain date and has promised faithfully to pass on the message. Ten to one the person will be
out or in a meeting when you call. Interviews arranged
with secretaries are usually acceptable, but make sure you
confirm them, preferably in writing.

■ **Don't be put off by people who are too busy.** Busy people can
always make time if they want to — push for ten minutes at
nine o'clock or five o'clock. Offer a bite to eat; busy people
must take sustenance.

■ **The respondent is always in a meeting when you phone.** Find
out from a secretary or a colleague when is the best time to
phone. Often it is first thing in the morning. This costs
more in telephone calls but is better than many fruitless
calls at the cheaper rate.

■ **The respondent says the sponsor already knows all there is to
know.** Explain that you are taking a rather special slant
and are looking at a particular aspect of the market that
has not been covered before.

■ **The respondent wants to know what sort of questions you will**

be asking. When setting up a face-to-face interview, try not to get down to detail on the telephone. This invites the respondent to say, 'I can't tell you that' or 'I don't know'. Talk in broad terms, for example, 'I will be asking general questions on the type of cable you buy.'

■ **The respondent asks you to send a questionnaire through the post and promises faithfully to return it.** Experience shows this approach seldom works. Explain that the question-naire has not been designed for self-completion and it just is not possible for the respondent to complete it unless you are there to help.

■ **The respondent is always being pestered by interviewers and what will the company get out of it?** Say the interview won't take long, that you think it will be an interesting exercise and, it is hoped, will help a supplier become more efficient in supplying goods to end-users, such as the respondent. Sell the respondent a benefit so that he really does feel that he is getting something out of taking part. Only offer pay-ments as a last resort. Payment for interviews in the long run works to the disadvantage of market researchers as they raise the costs of surveys and introduce bias in attract-ing mercenary (and possibly untypical) respondents.

With the best will in the world, some of the confirmed visits will be cancelled due to last-minute illness, crises, or plain forgetful-ness of the respondent. For this reason it can be prudent to book one or two more interviews than are required in the knowledge that some will not happen.

▥

GROUP DISCUSSIONS (FOCUS GROUPS) — WHEN AND WHERE TO USE THEM

■

GROUP DISCUSSIONS AND WHEN TO USE THEM

Group discussions (or focus groups) are a widely used fieldwork technique in consumer studies and they are playing an increasing role in business-to-business research. Group discussions are a meeting of a small number of respondents, typically 6 to 12. The respondents recruited for the groups are relevant to the study, for example:

■ They are in the target group of sex/age/social class of the study.
■ They are buyers of a certain product.
■ They are drawn from a particular occupation or profession (usually relevant in industrial market research).

Having been persuaded to attend, the group members meet and discuss areas of interest to the research. An interviewer acts as group leader or moderator. The meetings last one hour upwards with the proceedings recorded on audio tape (video recordings can also be used). For a particular project a number of groups are usually held, perhaps covering between them a spread of respondents and geographic areas.

This, then, is the bare bones of what is involved. Why are groups used so frequently in market research?

Group discussions are first and foremost a qualitative technique providing insights and allowing respondents' ideas and attitudes to be explored and understood. Here are four examples:

1. *Understanding consumer reactions to various types of floor covering:* A Swedish company wished to sell polished wooden flooring in the UK. The key question was: How to present this product to consumers?

   Consumers' perceptions of polished wooden floors needed to be compared and contrasted with attitudes to other floorings.

   Quantification of the market was *not* a priority. The company knew, for example, that the predominant floor covering in UK living rooms was wall-to-wall carpeting. What was needed was to understand *why* this was the case and *how* polished wooden floors could take a share of the market.

2. *Testing reactions to 'health food crisps':* Potato crisps enjoy a large and well established market in the UK. A manufacturer of crisps was concerned that the health food trend would eventually affect his market since crisps may be thought of as unhealthy, containing high quantities of sodium and fat. Could crisps, with some modification, be positioned as a health food?

   The requirement was, therefore, to understand how consumers would react to the concept of 'health food crisps'.

3. *Advertisement testing:* An advertising agency was asked to develop a new campaign for a building society. The key objective was to increase consumer awareness and confidence in a smaller society.

   TV advertising was proposed and an advertisement created to a point where there was a script and 'story board'. The advertising agency and its client wished to test out the theme, a 'then and now' story contrasting the change over 120 years since the society was founded.

   The advertisement, it was hoped, would be a successful

vehicle for confidence and awareness building. Would consumers see it in this way?

4. *Reactions of electricians to a new type of cable pack:* To improve production efficiency, a cable manufacturer wished to re-package house wiring cable in a new pack which, in outward appearance at least, differed considerably from the reel which had been used for decades.

It was hoped that as a by-product of using the new pack some marketing advantages would be gained. However, the bottom line was that electricians had merely to tolerate the new pack (ie not switch brands to the competition because of their dislike for it).

The cable manufacturers' sales and marketing staff recognised that they had very little detailed understanding of *how* electricians used cable and what their attitudes were to packaging.

Prototypes of the new pack were made available for research and the electricians' reactions to the new product were required.

The four cases outlined above are all very different in both subject and possible objectives for the research. In each case the group discussion technique was used and proved effective. What are the common themes here which favoured using groups?

In each case, to a greater or lesser extent, it was necessary to find out *consumer perceptions and attitudes*. We really don't know what consumers think about floor coverings, a 'healthy' crisp or building societies and we don't understand how electricians work with cable packs. In other words, we don't know the pertinent areas or attitudes to probe.

In order to obtain any real feedback, respondents needed quite a lot of information. In two or three cases it was necessary to *show a physical product*: descriptions and illustrations of flooring samples, perhaps samples of 'healthy' crisps, illustrations of the building society's proposed advert, and examples of the new cable pack.

Rather than merely obtaining simple measures of attitudes, it was necessary to understand in some depth how consumers think and feel about the products. A simple quantification is not enough. It may be that only five per cent of consumers are interested in 'healthy' crisps, but what sort of 'healthy' crisps would attract them and how should they be presented? Perhaps the majority of electricians dislike the new pack but is this dislike so strong that they will buy an alternative brand?

Groups discussions meet these requirements and therefore offer a very useful technique in qualitative research. There are, however, drawbacks and limitations.

First, to mention the most obvious, groups are a qualitative and not a quantitative research technique. If we need to ask 'how many' type questions, we should almost certainly be using another technique.

In a project we may need both qualitative and quantitative research. In the example of the new cable pack, we may find, perhaps, that the new pack is acceptable to all electricians except those who handle existing reels in a certain way — rolling them along the floor when paying out the cable, for example. The group discussion showed that only one or two electricians laid out cable in this way. How common is it generally, however? Perhaps a quantitative survey is required.

The reason why groups are not capable of yielding quantitative information is really twofold. First, by definition the samples are small, for example, four groups are typical for a study and this covers only 30 or so respondents. Second, the actual form of a group does not lend itself to precise quantification of data — there is general discussion, perhaps even boisterous argument, and this is difficult to translate into measurable responses.

Another feature of groups is the high element of subjectivity in handling and interpreting them. The outcome depends very much on the group leader and how he or she structures the discussion, conducts the meeting and analyses and interprets the results.

There is some element of subjectivity in all research but it is particularly noticeable in group discussion work. If the same brief is given to two experienced group researchers there is a chance that to some extent the outcome will differ. Obviously this is far from the scientific approach to quantitative research, where the interviewer's personality is expected to have no effect on the outcome.

A client commissioning group discussions should recognise

that the outcome will reflect the views of the respondents *and the researcher* in some unidentifiable mixture. For this reason there has to be every confidence in the ability and skill of the researcher. It is not only important that clients recognise this point, but that the researcher does as well.

The sample, coupled with this subjectivity, makes group discussion very suspect to some more quantitative-minded researchers. However, 'head counters' too must recognise the limitations of their own techniques, particularly the impossibility of answering the many 'how' and 'why' questions which are vital in marketing. Perhaps we can show through a survey that an advertisement fails to build awareness, but *why* is this the case? A particular formulation of 'healthy' crisps is unacceptable to its target market, but would small changes lead to a real winner?

12

CARRYING OUT EFFECTIVE GROUP DISCUSSIONS

■

PLANNING GROUPS

To be successful, groups need careful and thorough planning. The actual meeting may last only an hour or so but a lot of work has to be put in both beforehand as well as afterwards.

Some critical aspects of planning groups include:

- defining the compositions of the group;
- deciding the number of groups;
- planning the topics to be covered in the groups;
- organising the recruitment;
- choosing and booking the venue;
- making sure all equipment and 'props' are available;
- the timing of groups.

THE GROUP COMPOSITION

The characteristics of the respondents attending the groups have to relate to the aims and objectives of the research. This can be illustrated by returning to the four case studies used in the previous chapter.

- **Floorings.** Polished wood is a relatively expensive method of covering a floor and once laid is permanent. Consequently, the group respondents recruited for this group should be in above-average income jobs. Secondly, the manufacturer of this type of flooring has found that in Germany, the product appeals to the younger, more affluent segment of the population. It is thought that both men and women will be involved in a purchase decision and therefore both sexes should be included in the groups with a predominance of younger ages.

The group composition, therefore, can be defined in *demographic* terms.

■ **'Health food' crisps.** In this case the requirement is to convince groups of consumers with a health food interest. This might be defined by asking some questions to establish basic attitudes to health foods.

Group composition in this case is therefore defined in terms of *attitudes*.

■ **Building society advertisements.** The primary target here is adults who save to any extent. The group composition in this case is defined by *behaviour* and at the recruitment stage questions might be asked to establish if and where people save.

■ **Cable and pack electricians.** The need here is to include in the group actual *users* of cable — hands-on electricians. Recruitment is by membership *status* or responsibility. This sort of criterion is very common in industrial market research groups.

Group composition can be defined, therefore, in terms of demographics, attitudes or beliefs, behaviour or membership status. Fairly often, a combination of criteria is appropriate.

At the stage of planning the composition of the groups it is useful to consider the degree to which it is possible to recruit and convene the type of people required. Generally, in consumer research there are no insurmountable barriers to recruitment, although obviously the criteria used can make the group harder or easier to find. In industrial groups the potential members may be very thin on the ground or far apart (if members of a specialised profession and so on). Sometimes it may be impossible to convene the desired group, especially if there are few target respondents and they are scattered across the country.

DECIDING THE NUMBER OF GROUPS

Groups typically include only eight to nine respondents, so four groups provide a small sample of 32 to 36 respondents. However, as discussed earlier, groups are not meant to be a quantitative research tool and the limitations of small samples should be accepted.

If groups are to be a 'stand-alone' research technique, then four is probably the minimum number to hold. Groups can, however, be used at the 'exploratory' stage of the research; for example, as an aid to designing an effective questionnaire in a later quantitative stage. In this situation two or even one group may be adequate.

The composition planned for the groups is relevant to the number held. On the whole, groups can be seen to work best when the members are relatively homogenous. For example, in a consumer research project, it may be desirable to cover a spectrum of social classes and a wide range of ages as well as both sexes. In this case it is probably best to limit each group to a fairly narrow range, eg one group of lower income males aged 25–45; one of older, higher income men etc. If this principle is followed it has obvious implications for the number of groups held (assuming two income/status bands, two age ranges and both sexes, the minimum number of groups to cover all relevant respondents, is eight).

In the main, the argument in favour of homogenous groups is also apparent in business-to-business market research. In the construction industry, for example, it may be better to separate specifiers (architects, engineers) from materials buyers/users (builders and the building trade) and, again, this will be a factor in deciding the number of groups to hold.

The principle of homogenous groups is not immutable and there may be particular reasons to aim for a mix of respondents if an element of conflicting opinion would help flush out the contrasting views.

TOPIC PLANNING

In another book in this series, *Questionnaire Design*, you will find suggestions on how to prepare checklists for group discussions. This is the 'script' the group leader will use when leading the group. This checklist should include:

■ Notes on how the subject is to be introduced, eg:
   'We are carrying out research into roof insulation material. I understand you are all involved in this type of work and over the next hour or so I am interested in hearing your views on insulation material.'
■ The topics to be covered during the group. These will probably be in the form of questions and grouped in some form of sequence.
■ Notes to remind the group leader when to show visual aids etc.
■ Notes on when respondents are to do particular things — complete mini-questionnaires, write something out, draw pictures etc.

In a successfully led group, time is always short, and to ensure everything is covered it may be useful to have a timetable noted against the topics.

Group checklists are similar in many ways to questionnaires. There are, however, some important differences:

■ In a formal questionnaire the order of questions is pre-determined. In group discussions the dynamics of the meeting will be at least as strong an influence on topic order as the initial checklist. In other words, there is no need to stick to the checklist order.
■ Questions in a questionnaire are carefully formulated and worded and the interviewer is expected simply to read them as written. This is not the normal practice in a group where the moderator creates questions on the spot to suit the circumstances.
■ Often in a questionnaire the responses are pre-coded. This is never the case in a group.

At this point it is worth mentioning that formal questionnaires may be used as *part* of a group. Group members may, for example, fill in a self-completion questionnaire before, during or after the group meeting. The purpose of this may be to obtain simple, factual information about respondents and their behaviour.

ORGANISING THE RECRUITMENT

The next major section of this chapter is devoted to group recruitment, and the relevant points about organising this very important part of group discussion work are covered here. Indeed, all other aspects of planning the groups will be wasted if insufficient thought and effort are put into recruitment. A group can be led badly or well and cover the required information or not. The group cannot be held at all, however, if the recruitment falls down.

THE VENUE

Within reason, a group can be held more or less anywhere. However, a well-chosen venue will help the meeting go well and may affect attendance.

Consumer groups are perhaps best held in private homes. If an interviewer (rather than a researcher) does the recruitment, the venue may be her own home. Private homes generally seem more relaxing, particularly if the respondents are unfamiliar with attending meetings in hotels. However, it may not be practical to hold the meeting in a private home, and a small hotel or (in the UK) a room in a public house can be used successfully for consumer groups. Business-to-business research groups are invariably held in hotels.

There is an increasing trend to holding groups in places with special viewing facilities. These venues are often houses which have been converted for the express purpose of holding groups and they are equipped with one way mirrors. These enable a number of people to view the proceedings whilst being themselves hidden from view. The rooms have the advantage of being fitted out with video cameras and audio equipment and are excellent for capturing the results on tape. Clients like them because they can relax and watch the proceedings without being conspicuous. If the groups are held in more conventional surroundings, such as the recruiter's home, the observer has to sit in the wings. (My own experience is however that it is more disturbing to people to know that they are being watched from behind a mirror than to have someone sitting quietly in the same room).

Ideally, the researcher should check out the venue personally before booking. Second best is relying on the judgement of a colleague or associate, and as a last resort, probe the venue management over the phone to check out its suitability.

Here are a few guidelines to selecting the venue:

■ **Location.** It should be easy to find. The last thing you want is to lose respondents because they cannot find the venue. An hotel on a main road is usually better than one up a back street.

■ **Car parking.** If you expect respondents to come by car, the car parking facilities should be adequate. For this reason, a well-known city centre hotel can be a worse choice than one which is less well-known but a mile out of town.

■ **Access to the meeting room.** If you need to use sizeable equipment or show product samples, it is worth checking out how possible it is to get a vehicle close to the room. (This became very apparent in a project which involved carrying 40 reels of cable into each meeting room.)

■ **Room size.** Get this right and avoid rooms which are either too small or too large.

■ **Furnishings.** The group can meet either round a table or sit more informally in a loose circle. A table is rather a formal arrangement and more appropriate for business-to-business research groups than for consumers. Either way, make sure there are enough chairs.

■ **Power supply.** If you are relying on mains for your tape recorder or video, etc you will almost certainly find the socket is in the wrong place. Take an extension cable with you.

■   **Ambience.** An attractive venue may be some encouragement to attendance and different ambiences will be suited
to different classes of respondent.

EQUIPMENT AND PROPS

The only important point here is to make sure everything you
need is available on the night and that there is some back-up.

Groups are invariably recorded, so make sure the tape recorder
is available and that there are enough blank tapes. Tape recorders
break down and tapes are not faultless so there should be at least
a second tape recorder available and to be really sure, a second
recording should be taken.

If you are showing product samples or advertising visuals,
impress on those who are supplying them that they have to be
ready on time — and that does not mean half an hour before the
first group arrives. Advertising agencies can be shockers in this
respect.

Don't assume that some important prop will be available at the
venue without checking first. If you need a stand for a video camera,
take one with you.

TIME AND DATES

Generally, both consumer and industrial research groups are
held in the evening, from 7 pm onwards. Other times of the day,
however, can sometimes work; perhaps the afternoon, for consumer respondents without jobs, or lunchtime for business-to-
business groups (some business respondents find a plausible
excuse for a couple of hours away from work is a positive
attraction).

Friday is not a good day to hold groups since there are likely to
be quite a few counter-attractions to attendance. Otherwise any
weekday seems as good as another. Group discussions are not
usually held at weekends, although there is no reason why not
other than (perhaps) the fact that moderators prefer their weekends to be free.

RECRUITING GROUPS

Group leaders often underestimate the effort put into recruitment because they are not personally involved. Only when the magic eight respondents fail to materialise does the group leader become interested in this side of the work. The do-it-yourself researcher cannot avoid the problems of recruitment since he will be doing the work or working very closely with those who are.

The aim of the group recruitment is very simple: *to have the right number of qualified respondents attend at the right time.* Who is qualified is determined by the group composition criteria and obviously recruitment cannot start until this is settled. There is, however, another 'qualification' issue which should be mentioned; this is the problem of 'professional' group respondents — respondents who repeatedly attend groups. This problem can arise when a recruiter is tempted to invite respondents who have attended other groups recently. This can be overcome by stipulating that respondents should not have attended a group in the last 6, 12 or 24 months, or whatever is thought reasonable.

Some general principles which apply to both business-to-business and consumer groups are:

■ In group recruitment you have to contact and screen more potential respondents than will actually attend the group. Some people who are approached will not qualify for attendance while others will be unavailable or unwilling. The ratio of contacts to attendees varies according to the type of respondent, the subject of the group etc. A 5:1 ratio should be regarded as optimistic and perhaps 10:1 as a safe working assumption in an 'average group'.

■ Potential respondents need to be persuaded to give up time to attend and the recruiter needs to 'sell' the group. The rewards offered may include:

— An interesting and enjoyable meeting — respondents should feel the hour is going to be agreeably spent.
— Tangible benefits at the venue — drinks and snacks.
— Some handouts to take away — it is normal to give

respondents an incentive. A bottle of spirits is often a suitable 'thank you' for business-to-business respondents but if money is more appropriate, then it should approximate to twice the value of a bottle of malt if it is to be seen as worthwhile. Consumer respondents tend to react best to a cash incentive equal to about a bottle of spirits. If budgets allow, the researcher may be tempted to give a larger incentive and occasionally this may be judged necessary.

— Altruistic rewards such as: 'The research will help a manufacturer improve his service to customers.' Perhaps both recruiter and respondent feel better if this is said, although it is doubtful that the appeal cuts much ice.

■ While the recruiter needs to 'sell' the group, it is dangerous to be over-pushy. Most potential respondents can be persuaded to *say* they will come to the group but whether they actually turn up is a different matter. Over-persuasion leads to promises which don't materialise and a poorly attended group. If the respondent seems at all uncertain or hesitant it is probably better to try someone else. You have to aim for a genuine 'cross my heart and hope to die' promise.

■ Unless they have attended a group before (and you may be at pains to make sure they haven't), potential respondents are likely to be uncertain and anxious about the purpose of the meeting. Fears may include that they will be sold something, that the event will be of dubious propriety, or that they will be 'tested' in some way. Such fears are not easy to allay. However, the recruiter needs to explain the purpose of the group simply and pre-empt the objections:

'I am asking a few people who save to look at some new advertisements for a building society so that we can choose the best one. We just want you to see the adverts and give us your opinion. You will find it quite fun really.'

'I want to stress that I am not trying to sell anything; the meeting is for market research purposes only.'

■ Start the recruitment in good time but not too early. Initial contact with respondents is often best made about a week before the group date, although if the respondents are senior professionals, a longer lead time may be needed to win a slot in their diaries.

■ Recruitment is a multi-stage process. As a minimum, the initial contact and promise to attend should be followed up with a mailed invitation plus a further reminder (perhaps by phone) on the day or the evening before.

■ Make sure the respondents know when and where the group is being held. The written invitation card should clearly state the time (eg 7.15 pm for 7.30 pm) and how to find the location of the place where it is being held.

■ Except where the recruitment criteria are very simple (eg age, sex) it is good practice for the recruiter to complete a simple questionnaire for each respondent promising to attend. This may include questions designed to check the qualifications of the respondent (attitudes to a subject, personal status, shopping patterns etc), a question to exclude those who have recently attended a group as well as contact information (name, address, phone number etc).

■ A final general principle is *fear the worst* and assume that every respondent won't turn up on the night. Consumer attendees are usually very good at turning up and if nine are recruited than it is almost certain that eight or nine will turn up. In business-to-business groups the situation is rather different and there is a need to over-recruit; 12 to 14 firm promises will generate around eight or nine respondents on the night. At worst, it is usually possible to fit a couple of extra respondents into the meeting rather than send them away disgruntled after they have gone to some trouble to get there.

RECRUITING CONSUMER GROUPS

In consumer group recruitment, the initial contact with potential respondents is usually carried out in the home, sometimes in the street. The recruiter/interviewer approaches apparently relevant respondents and establishes whether they are qualified and willing to attend the group. It is best to check the qualifications first and for this only a brief introduction is likely to be needed, such as:

'My name is xxx of xxx. I am carrying out some market research. Could I please ask you a few very short questions?'

The recruitment questionnaire is then used or questions are otherwise asked to check qualifications. Only if the respondent is qualified does the recruiter/interviewer introduce the group meeting.

'Thank you very much. At present I am inviting a small number of people to attend a short meeting. This is to obtain people's views about xxx.'

'I must stress this is just for research purposes. We are not selling anything and I am sure you will enjoy it.'

'By the way, we are giving people who come xxx.'

'Will you come?'
(IF YES/POSSIBLE)

'The meeting will be on xxx at 7 pm. It is being held at xxx. Can you make it then?'
(IF YES)

'Thank you very much.'

'We aim to have a meeting of eight people so it is very important to me that you come.'

'I will contact you again nearer the time.'
(OBTAIN ADDRESS/PHONE NUMBER)

A written invitation can be given out there and then or sent later. In the suggested introduction it will be noted that at the end there is some pressure for commitment. This is important as it is better to try another potential respondent than to have a doubtful promise.

┌─────────────── **invitation** ───────────────┐

we shall be pleased to see you at our
Market Research Group Discussion

on _____ at _____

the meeting will be held at

_____

_____

_____

Please contact the person overleaf or our office if you are unable to attend

The Court High Lane, Stockport SK6 8DX.
Telephone: Disley (0663) 765115

✓ BUSINESS
& MARKET
RESEARCH PLC

└──┘

Figure 12.1 Group discussion invitation card

Consumer group recruitment is generally done on a house-to-house basis or on the phone, the latter being especially relevant when there is a specific list of individuals who need inviting (for example, members of a society). Occasionally, the recruitment takes place in the street. For 'difficult' groups where the relevant criteria suggest a 'needle in a haystack' approach, informal referrals may be used — one respondent suggesting another who fits the bill.

The initial recruitment should be regarded only as a first stage and it is desirable to assume up to 100 per cent drop out (ie, recruit 16 to obtain 8 respondents). The recruitment should be followed up, ideally by visiting the respondent's home. The 'excuse' of this follow-up visit can be to hand over the written invitation personally. The fact that the recruiter has gone to the trouble of visiting the respondent increases their commitment to attend and the opportunity should be taken to seek verbal reassurance on this point.

Commitment at this stage should reduce the drop-out rate but it may still be prudent to assume some promises will not be kept (perhaps 12 promises to the required eight respondents).

It is worth going to the third recruitment stage, with a phone call the night before or even early the same evening as the group meeting. By this stage probably nothing can be done to replace drop-outs but at least you have a better idea of the likely attendance. Even now don't count on 100 per cent turn-out (perhaps 9 or 10 promises to 7 or 8 attendances). The whole recruitment process might stretch to a week.

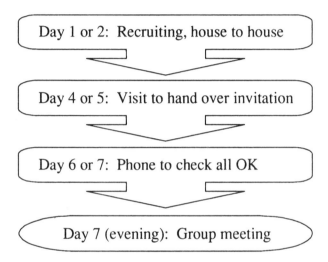

Figure 12.2 Timetable for group recruitment

RECRUITING BUSINESS-TO-BUSINESS GROUPS

The basic strategy of recruitment is no different for consumer and business-to-business groups. In both, recruitment is in a number of stages, with each seeking to increase the respondent's level of commitment.

Obviously, house-to-house or street interviewing is not appropriate in business-to-business group recruitment and the normal approach is by phone. Industrial group respondents are usually selected on the grounds of occupation/business classification and the first step is to draw up, from a trade directory or similar source, a list of relevant businesses in the district where the group is being held. The distance over which respondents can be successfully recruited varies but on the whole it is best to assume that respondents will not spend more than half an hour travelling.

On making contact with a qualified individual, exactly the same approach can be used as for the recruitment of consumer respondents:

1. A short explanation that research is being carried out.
2. Initial screening questions to confirm whether or not the individual qualifies.
3. The group is introduced.
4. An invitation is offered.
5. Any incentives are offered.
6. A firm commitment is sought.

Again, the final emphasis should be on getting a definite undertaking to attend, even at the expense of 'frightening off' the lukewarm.

If the respondents are drawn locally, the second stage of recruitment, as for consumer groups, can be a visit to hand over the written invitation. Wherever this is possible, it is worth doing; face-to-face contact undoubtedly increases commitment. However, the distances involved often make visits impractical.

The alternative to visits is a mailed invitation and it is worth having a quality card specially printed for the particular group. It should not be left at that, however; a telephone call should follow. The purpose of this second call is to:

1. check that the invitation has been received.
2. resolve any doubts, queries and misconception the respondent may have (he fears that this is a disguised sales pitch, he doesn't 'know' enough etc).
3. press for commitment.

Undoubtedly by this stage there will have been some fall-out and there may be still time for last minute replacements.

The third stage of the recruitment, a final phone reminder, should be made the day before or on the day of the meeting.

On the whole, attendance at business-to-business groups is

more chancy than for consumer groups. Last-minute business 'emergencies' prevent respondents attending. Also, at least some groups of business respondents are more likely to give insincere commitments; they promise to attend because it is easier than saying no. To some extent this problem can be reduced by giving every opportunity for refusal in the early stage of recruitment.

The likelihood of some drop-out *must* be anticipated and for a group of eight, firm promises from 12 should be the objective at the last stage of recruitment, with perhaps 20 promises at the first stage.

HOW TO LEAD GROUPS

When it comes to leading groups, interviewers are very much on their own. However, an assistant is useful, although not essential, to see to some of the mundane tasks connected with the venue and, above all, host the respondents. This involves welcoming them to the venue, keeping them happy until the group starts and handing out the incentives at the end.

It is advisable to arrive at the venue in good time so that any equipment can be set up and furniture moved, well before the first respondents show up. Check the tape recorder and ideally run two simultaneously. If the venue is a hotel, make sure the staff understand the catering requirements. Have drinks and snacks set out before the group starts as there is nothing worse than being interrupted half-way through.

The ten minutes or so before the start of the group is particularly stressful for the moderator because of the inevitable uncertainty about attendance. One problem may be deciding when to start. If at the appointed time the attendance is poor, the moderator is faced with the dilemma of waiting in the hope of late arrivals (there usually are some) or risking restlessness among those who have turned up. When it is judged that the time is right, the respondents should be brought into the room (if they are not already there) and settled down with refreshments.

Once the group is seated, the proceedings commence with a welcome and a short introduction about the purpose of the group. At this point respondents may still feel anxious, uncertain and perhaps suspicious about the real purpose of the meeting. A short, light-hearted welcome and introduction will start to lower the barriers.

The group proceedings have to be recorded and respondents should (on ethical grounds) be told that this is happening. Don't, however, make a big issue out of this and don't ask if anyone objects — what do you do if someone does?

Make it clear that over the next hour or so, the group is expected to talk while you listen and then get some immediate involvement by having each respondent introduce him or herself. This might be their name and involvement in the subject of the discussion (eg use of a particular product, a particular job and so on).

The group is now primed and ready. How should the moderator make it all work? Two general points concern planning and the leader's own attitudes.

Clearly the moderator must know in detail what subjects are to be covered. A discussion guide will have been prepared with the topics arranged in a logical order. It is important that the moderator is totally familiar with all the topics so that it is possible to jump around in any order as the need arises. If during the group the last topic on the list is raised early, it can be brought forward.

Another aspect of running the groups is to have a plan which anticipates the *pace* of the discussion. This avoids the possibility of covering half the topics extensively with insufficient time for the rest. The moderator must be prepared to move the discussion on ruthlessly to keep to the schedule. Don't assume that the meeting can be prolonged. Someone may have a real reason for finishing promptly and once one goes, all the other respondents will start itching to leave as well.

The moderator's own attitudes will mould, manoeuvre and lead the group. However, *the group is not an ego trip for its leader.* On the transcript, the moderator's input should be only one tenth, possibly one twentieth, of the total. The moderator must also be wary of projecting views and attitudes on to the group. Undoubtedly, the moderator has some opinions on the subject but these must be kept hidden. Any obvious bias will either produce a group which is in agreement or one which has a strong anti-reaction. It is also desirable that the moderator makes this impartiality clear. If, for example, the subject of the group is a new project concept, it should be emphasised that both praise and criticism of the product is welcome as long as the respondents express their own beliefs honestly.

Now we move on to the techniques of 'leading' the group.

LEADER INITIATIVES

The direct question

The simplest stimulus is the direct question:

■ How often do you buy cable?
■ What does the headline (in an advertisement) mean?
■ Which foods are particularly bad for you?

There is nothing wrong at all with direct questions and probably most moderators' input is of this type. The key, however, is to use questions which invite a discursive response and in general to avoid those which simply require an answer 'yes' or 'no'.

A problem with direct questions is that they invite respondents to answer one by one and respond to the group leader rather than entering into a discussion. However, a response to a direct question can be followed up by inviting others to comment:

Leader: 'Which foods are particularly bad for you?'
Respondent: 'Well, I think salt's a real killer.'
Leader: 'What do the rest of you think of that?'

Giving information

An advantage of the group is that the moderator can not only give information, but correct misconceptions as they arise. Firstly, the moderator is watching out for any spontaneous mention of the subject matter. Thereafter, information may be disclosed bit by bit, verbally to start with and then showing an illustration, a concept board or the product itself.

In giving information, two pitfalls to avoid are devoting too much time to the explanation (ie curtailing the discussion itself) and 'overselling'.

The challenge

A useful technique is the challenge. This is particularly appropriate when the responses seem rather one-sided. The challenge may be to the prevailing wisdom by putting the contrary view or pointing out logical inconsistencies in the views exposed.

> 'You all say that fitted carpets make for a clean house. I have heard said that carpets are dirt traps. What do you say to that?'

> 'You all say you buy insulation mats on price, yet you hardly ever shop around. If you don't compare prices, how can you claim to buy on price?'

Asking respondents to put forward a view

A useful technique is to ask a respondent to put forward some views for others to discuss:

> 'Perhaps you can tell us of some situations where you would use this . . .?'

This approach encourages the group members to participate, which is the object of a group discussion.

An extension is to ask a respondent who has proved a forceful exponent of a particular view to put forward the contrary argument:

> 'You seem very sceptical about this new product. Just suppose, however, you had to argue in its favour — what points would you make?'

Role playing

A variant of the previous technique is to get respondents to act out roles. Here a respondent (or half the group) is invited to 'sell' the new product and the rest to be reluctant customers. Equally, respondents may be asked to role-play an abstract concept:

'Imagine in a play you had to represent Brand X breakfast food. What would you say? Show us.'

A good rule in group discussions is to be flexible and responsive. If a particular technique is not working, try something else.

Questionnaire or list completion

Asking respondents to complete a questionnaire can be a useful part of a group. The questionnaire might include a scale:

Assuming the new pack was the same price as a standard reel, how likely would you be to accept it?

- very likely
- fairly likely
- uncertain
- fairly unlikely
- very unlikely.

Having a questionnaire completed in this way can flush out views before they get distorted by those of others, and enables attitudes to be quantified (although the small sample size involved may make this of limited value).

As well as completed questionnaires, group respondents can write lists of other things, for example suggestions for a new brand name.

Questionnaire completion or list writing can be an aid to discussion. Respondents are asked to read out their responses and comment on those of each other. Remember, however, that the point of a group is for *discussion* and the time taken to complete questionnaires etc should be kept to a minimum. Basic factual information about the respondent is best obtained at the recruitment stage or perhaps on a self-completion basis just before the group starts.

Doing other things

As well as talking and writing, group members can be involved in other activities. They can, for example, demonstrate using a tool or material (eg show how a cable reel is unwound). Acting may be a part of role playing and drawing can provide useful insights to attitudes and feelings.

FACING PROBLEMS

Problems can arise in the group session, the most worrying of which is the *non-talkative group*. Here the group says very little, offering only short answers to direct questions. In all probability the right stimulus is not being used. Some ways of dealing with the problem include:

■ Make sure the group understands the purpose of the meeting; that research and not a sales pitch is involved. Lack of communication may reflect anxiety and suspicion.
■ Tell the group they are *expected* to talk.
■ Try different techniques: challenges, giving information, role playing etc, instead of direct questions.
■ Change the topic. Perhaps the one which is sticking is uninteresting to the group. It is always possible to return to it when the session hots up.

Another common problem is the *non-contributing* respondent. He or she sits in the corner and says nothing, usually because of timidity and shyness. The group leader has to make a special effort to involve the respondent. The use of the respondent's first name can be welcoming (a reason for noting names at the start of the session). To some extent this problem is found in all groups and the moderator needs to watch out continually for the non-contributor. Of course, the level of participation from respondents cannot be equal, or even nearly so, but an eight-strong group with real contributions from only four is not satisfactory.

The opposite problem is the *over-talkative* respondent who dominates the discussion. This problem can be partly overcome by the moderator encouraging others to talk. However, the over-talkative person may have to be positively discouraged, very firmly if necessary. Usually this type of person is pretty thick-skinned and can take quite rough treatment.

A related problem is the *joker*. Some humour and light heartedness invariably helps a group's running, but the respondent with a quip for everything rapidly loses his charm. Comedians feed on their audience's laughter and a stone-faced reaction to the next gag usually solves the problem.

Often in a session the group can become *side-tracked* and start discussing something quite irrelevant. Don't be deluded that some startling deep insights will be revealed. Once side-tracked, the group is likely to talk on indefinitely and the key topics will not be covered. By all means let the group ramble briefly, even at the cost of some irrelevance, but not for more than a minute or so. Bring them back to the point.

These, then, are some problems which may have to be faced in running a group. The moderator must be sensitive to these and other problems and continually monitor how the session is going. A group should be enjoyable both for the leader and respondents. The moderator readily recognises a group which is going well from the intangible 'dynamic' created by the positive gelling of 8 or 9 different personal chemistries.

A final tip is to leave the tape recorder running after bringing the session to an end. In the final minutes afterwards, respondents can make some very interesting 'off the record' comments.

13

HALL TESTS AND CLINICS

■

Like group discussions, hall tests and clinics involve recruiting respondents to attend a venue but unlike groups, such research is usually quantitative, involving sizeable samples of respondents.

The term 'hall tests' is largely confined to applications in consumer market research and 'clinics' for the industrial or business-to-business field. However, the two terms are often used loosely and interchangeably.

A feature common to hall tests and clinics is that they cannot be carried out practically on a 'one-man' basis. A team has to be involved in recruitment and interview administration. However, an in-house researcher can certainly organise an exercise of this type if there is access to an interviewing team.

HALL TESTS

Hall tests involve *recruiting* a respondent sample, bringing them into a *venue* (the hall) and administering *interviews*. Each of these aspects is discussed below. First, however, we consider why and where hall tests are used.

THE AIMS OF HALL TESTS

Central to the purpose of holding a hall test is the need to show something to respondents. Usually this is a product, so hall tests and product testing are often regarded as synonymous — although this is not necessarily the case. Hall tests are also used to test packs and advertising material.

When a product is the subject of a hall test, the objective is usually to establish consumers' acceptance, preference and attitudes. Often the product is new and the respondents have not seen it in the shops. In most cases, reactions to the physical formulation of the product are required rather than attitudes to the brand. For these reasons the product test is often 'blind' with the respondents unaware of which brands are being tested.

In real life, products are bought in a context of choice. A person goes into a shop and chooses one chocolate bar rather than another. Product testing should normally, therefore, be comparative; the product being compared with other products which the new one will replace, perhaps against the leading competitive products.

Products tested in a hall should be capable of being evaluated in this artificial environment and most items of food and drink fall into this category. Eating a chocolate biscuit in a hall is no different from eating one at home. Similarly, products whose key characteristics can be seen or smelt or which can be used in a simple way, can all be objects of a hall test. Products inappropriate for hall tests include: personal hygiene products (eg deodorants), products which have to be used over time (eg a soap powder) or in a fairly complex way (eg a window cleaner), or those whose use would be simply impractical in the hall (eg shampoo). Similarly, products where a conditioning process is necessary to gain acceptance may not be suitable to hall tests and this presents problems for certain drinks and foodstuffs. For example, beers which tend towards the slightly sweet and slightly gassy score quite well in hall tests but they would rapidly loose appeal if drunk in quantity, night after night. When a hall test is not appropriate, it is necessary to consider testing the product in the normal place of consumption (the home, the pub etc).

Hall tests are a quantitative technique and when used in product testing the aim is to make specific measurements. Typically these include:

- **Acceptance.** Will the product be considered at all?
- **Preference.** Which product is preferred?
- **Attitudes to attributes.** A product can be considered as a collection of attributes: colour, texture, smell, taste etc (and each of these can be further subdivided). Attitudes on each can be measured, with satisfaction or preferences compared.

The end result of a product test should be to assist decisions. If it is a new product, how well is it accepted? How does it compare with established products? If an established product, how does it compare with its competitors? What are its strengths and weaknesses? Product testing is therefore diagnostic.

As well as product testing, hall tests are often used for pack testing. For many consumer products the pack is a major element within the purchasing decision. Indeed, it may be the only way in which it differs from competitive brands. Getting the pack right is therefore a critical factor.

Generally, pack tests are carried out for a new product or when an established product is being changed. Typically, the object is to compare a few possible pack designs, either with each other or with those of competitors. This is done by showing mock-ups which are as near the finished packs as possible. As in product testing, packs are tested for specific attributes — colour, legibility, perceived appropriateness to the product etc. The specific questions asked about the pack are structured and usually 'closed'. If required, any qualitative probing of the pack concept will have been carried out in group discussions prior to the hall test.

Hall tests also have a role in advertising research. Again, the aim is to obtain quantitative responses to specific aspects of an advertisement such as the impact of its headlines, communication or memorability of the copy and visuals etc. If the advertising medium covered is the press, a hall test might be used for speed and convenience although alternative methods could be chosen (eg home or even street interviewing). Other media, however, cannot be shown without bulky equipment (TV advertisements, posters etc), making a hall test approach essential.

VENUES

Choice of a suitable venue is a vital aspect of planning a hall test. The venue must be located suitably for respondent recruitment and, in the main, the recruitment of respondents for a hall test is invariably 'off the street'. For this reason the venue must be immediately adjacent to a busy pedestrian area, perhaps in a major town shopping street or precinct.

The room should be also easily accessible from the street; ideally straight off the street, through a door and into the room. Negotiating more than a single flight of stairs or using a lift will be off-putting to respondents, not to mention the research staff when setting up.

In most consumer research only small products are involved and these present no real problems when selecting a venue. Occasionally, larger products (eg domestic appliances, carpets etc) may be tested and possible access problems should be considered.

With some products, preparations may be required such as dispensing drinks, cutting up things, diluting, or perhaps heating up. A kitchen facility may therefore be needed as part of presenting the product. Even if this is not the case, it may be required to provide refreshments to respondents and research staff.

The room should be big enough for the anticipated number of respondents and research staff. A typical arrangement is for an interviewer to bring a respondent into the hall, show product samples and administer an interview. There should be sufficient space to do this without getting in the way of other interviewers and respondents. Ideally, respondents should not be able to overhear other respondents being interviewed elsewhere in the room and screens may be a help in this regard. In group discussion work, a venue can be too big. In hall tests a venue is only likely to be regarded as over-large on cost grounds.

Appropriate furniture is needed in the hall; tables on which to display products, chairs for respondents and interviewers, and perhaps screens. These must be arranged either independently or though the hall's management. Needless to say, the products to be tested must also be arranged in advance and available on the day. A new product may be specially prepared at the factory and the researcher's role is limited to ensuring that it is delivered on time. Any established products are bought in for the test.

Staffing required to recruit and interview respondents is discussed below. In addition, a hall test usually requires staff for support duties which include preparing test products, clearing up between respondents, preparing refreshments etc. The number of such helpers depends on the anticipated throughput and number of interviews involved. Perhaps one helper to four interviewers is a reasonable rule of thumb.

In planning a hall test, the proposed venue *must* be inspected before it is booked and the researcher in charge should check out the alternatives personally. A bad choice will have a serious effect.

RECRUITING

The almost universal method of hall test recruitment is on the street in the immediate vicinity of the hall. Respondents 'captured' are brought into the hall to participate in the research.

At the planning stage, decisions will be made on the demographic profile of the respondents and usually quotas are set to ensure a representative sample. The sex of the respondent will normally be determined by the nature of the product being studied. For a 'household' food item, housewives would normally be interviewed; for car products or beer, men; and for some household appliances, probably both sexes. The decision is based on knowledge or expectations of who buys the product.

Quite commonly, respondents are restricted to users of the product being researched. In a beer test, clearly it would be necessary to screen out teetotallers. The sample might also be stratified to include predetermined proportions of heavy, medium and light users of the product.

To aid recruitment, a questionnaire is essential. This is used in the street to establish whether potential respondents meet the recruitment criteria and it can be brought into the hall to follow the respondent through the test.

In initial contact with respondents, interviewers should be concerned only to establish if the respondent is qualified. Now, and only now, is the subject of the hall test introduced and an invitation extended to attend. Normally, the respondent is encouraged to proceed straight into the hall and it is best if the recruiting interviewer accompanies the respondent. Once inside, the recruiter can either hand over the respondent to an in-hall interviewer or play this part herself. On the whole, the latter approach seems to work best and avoids problems of interviewers either having nothing to do or being overwhelmed by a rush of respondents.

The number of respondents processed through the hall per day depends on a number of factors including:

■ The duration of the in-hall test and interview.
■ The number of recruiting and in-hall interviewers.
■ The level of pedestrian traffic immediately outside the hall. (If the venue has been carefully selected this should be not be a limiting factor.)

If it is assumed that each test will take around 10 to 15 minutes and that recruiters also act as in-hall interviewers, three respondents per hour per interviewer should be achievable — say 20 interviews a day. A team of five or six interviewers, with some additional helpers in the hall, could therefore process around 100 respondents per day though this should be considered good going. Involving more interviewers would not necessarily improve the numbers to any great extent as the law of diminishing returns will set in. For example, there may be problems in having too many interviewers attempting to recruit at once outside the hall. It may be better instead to have a smaller team and to run the hall test over two days.

To meet the needs of just one project, hall tests might have to be carried out in several towns seeking an overall sample of 500 or more. If only one town is used, there is a danger of reflecting local tastes in the results. In some product fields strong local or regional tastes could lead to a misleading national extrapolation.

Apart from perhaps a cup of tea and a biscuit, incentives are not usually required for street-recruited respondents.

Occasionally, street recruitment is inappropriate. Perhaps the target respondents are too thinly spread to obtain a large enough sample off the street. If this is the case, the recruiting methods for clinics (discussed later) will have to be considered.

IN THE HALL

What happens in the hall on the day of the test must, of course, be planned in detail beforehand, along with all other aspects of the work. For example, decisions have to made on the appropriate method of presenting test products to respondents. Similarly, a questionnaire has to be designed for the in-hall interview (and recruitment).

The need for recruitment interviewers (and whether they should also work as interviewers within the hall itself) has already been discussed, as has the need for support staff to carry out the various 'housekeeping' duties in the hall. An important additional member of the team is a supervisor. He or she should have nothing else to do but orchestrate the work of other staff and solve the numerous problems and temporary crises which always arise. The supervisor should also check over completed questionnaires, although it may be desirable to have someone acting as an on-the-spot checker/coder. This is particularly the case when results are required as quickly as possible — and with a personal computer in the hall itself, instant results at the end of the day are practical.

As already indicated, different approaches to presenting products tested in a hall can be considered. The products, for example, can be 'blind' or 'branded'. Normally, the point of the hall test is to obtain respondents' preferences and attitudes to a product *without* any influence from expectations of the brand name. If a new chocolate bar scores well against a competitor's product, we want to be sure that this reflects the product's attributes rather than any 'halo effect'. However, occasionally the reactions to an identified brand may be wanted, perhaps towards the end of the test and after the products have been tested blind.

If the test is to be blind, the brand name must be hidden or disguised. In some cases this is easy; the brand of a drink, for example, is not normally obvious unless the bottle is on show. With other products, however, obscuring the brand name may be difficult and require much ingenuity. Occasionally it will be impossible.

Obviously, in a blind test the products have to be labelled 'A', 'B' etc and care is needed by all concerned to ensure that the right product goes with the right label. Also, a point should be made of writing down the identity of the codes as a permanent record as it would be seriously embarrassing to forget later which was which.

Products or packs are usually tested in a comparative way. A new product, for example, may be tested against the brand leader or the manufacturer's established brand. Commonly this is done by *multiple* testing. Each respondent sees/tries each product and is questioned about each. By contrast, in *monadic* testing each respondent only sees/tries and is interviewed about one product. Any product comparisons made through monadic testing involve comparing the results from matched samples: 100 respondents, for example, test 'A' and matched by another 100 respondents — test 'B'. Multiple testing is more commonly used as it is easier and cheaper than monadic testing where twice the sample size is required. However, monadic testing may be preferred or be the only possible approach in some circumstances. It may, for example, only be possible for respondents to use a single product, or because of the nature of the product it may be impossible for them to distinguish a second product. Strong mint sweets, for example, cannot be satisfactorily tested in succession. Monadic tests are also more realistic because in reality we don't buy two products and try them out in immediate succession.

If a multiple test is used, order bias must be avoided. The results of a product test where 'A' is always tested before 'B' may be very different from one where 'B' is tested before 'A'. The problem is usually overcome by rotating the order of presentation. Detailed procedures should be set to ensure that this is achieved.

The questionnaire and questions used in a hall test depend on the objectives of the research and the nature of the product, pack or advertisement. In a product test of two orange juices, for example, relevant questions may include:

■   **Acceptance.** Would you describe the juice A/B (ROTATE) as:

   — excellent

— very good
— fairly good
— neither good nor poor
— fairly poor
— very poor
— terrible?

■ **Preference.** Of the two juices, which do you prefer for:

— colour
— the look of the liquid
— thickness of the liquid
— taste (this might be subdivided into various dimensions of taste)
— overall?

More diagnostic questions may also be included to establish why, for example, one juice is preferred to another, eg for thickness.

■ Would you say that juice A/B (ROTATE) is:

— much too thick
— a bit too thick
— about right
— a bit too thin
— much too thin?

In any objective test, the difference between two products tested may be marginal and quite possibly respondents will find it difficult to discriminate at all. This can be tested, for example, by having two juices labelled A, B, C and D, with A and C one juice and B and D the other. Respondents are asked to give a preference between A and B and then C and D. If there is true discrimination, the preference for A and C and for B and D should be the same.

As well as covering specific questions about the products being tested, the questionnaire may usefully include questions on use, purchase and attitudes in the relevant product field. In the analysis, the data obtained from such questions might then be related to the questions about the products themselves (eg stated brand preferences compared with preference expressed in the blind test).

Once the product test and interview are completed, the respondent may be offered refreshment and perhaps the chance to sit down before returning to the shopping trip. This is best arranged in a room or area away from the interviewing.

CLINICS

The term 'clinics' is used to refer to product tests where respondents are invited to a venue to comment on vehicles or business/industrial products. A very obvious difference between hall tests and clinics is in the nature of the products researched and in turn this has implications for the venue. The other major difference is associated with respondent recruitment as clinic respondents are not brought in off the street and the approach is much closer to that of group discussions.

In the remainder of this chapter the points of difference between clinics and hall tests are highlighted.

CLINIC AIMS

The basic aims of a clinic are likely to be the same as a hall test and with a need to *show* something, most often a product. In principle, almost any product can be shown although some may present insurmountable problems. For a product to be tested in a clinic, the key features to be researched must be apparent in some way. Possibly a product's key attribute is its longevity and reliability but if this cannot be 'seen' (and it usually cannot) respondent perceptions cannot be researched in a clinic.

One feature of the types of product commonly researched in clinics is that often they cannot be researched 'blind'. If the subject is trucks or cars, for example, it may be possible to disguise the brand (marque) of the prototype but not those of the competitive makes set against it.

As in hall tests, packs and advertising material rather than products can be the subject of a clinic and often research involving these is far more practical for a small research department than attempting to show relatively large and complex physical products.

VENUES

The nature of the products researched in a clinic may impose specific venue requirements. If the products are large and heavy, access to the room is a critical concern. Such special requirements mean that there are fewer venues in an area for clinics than for hall tests. Prior inspection is essential.

For really large products an alternative is an outside display which might be combined with some sort of demonstration. This method of research is subject to the vagaries of the weather as respondents cannot be expected to be diligent in their examination of the products from beneath umbrellas.

The other critical aspect of venue choice is its suitability for respondents. Respondents will have to make their own way to the venue and therefore:

- It should be easy to find.
- There should be adequate parking space.
- Preferably the venue should be attractive enough to be an incentive to attend.

The venue must also be located within an area with an adequate population of target respondents.

RECRUITMENT

In clinic work, respondents are usually defined in terms of their job or functional responsibility, for example:

- Owners of certain cars.
- Transport managers for a commercial vehicle hall test.
- Office managers for reprographic equipment.
- Building company buyers for construction equipment.

Such respondents cannot be recruited off the street immediately outside the clinic venue and, instead, the recruitment process is much the same as for groups but on a larger scale. In outline, the key steps are:

■ Building up a list of relevant respondents (companies) within the catchment area of a venue. As a rule of thumb, a half-hour car drive is the maximum limit to the catchment area. The distances involved, therefore, depend on the state of the roads.

■ Contacting the companies by phone to identify the relevant respondents.

■ Carrying out an initial telephone screening interview with the respondent.

■ Inviting the respondent to attend the clinic at a set time.

■ Sending a follow-up postal invitation (which includes directions to the clinic).

■ Making follow-up contacts by phone immediately before the clinic day.

After the initial contact list has been prepared, the recruitment process spans at least one week.

As for group discussions, some drop-outs must be expected; perhaps 25 to 40 per cent of the 'firm' promises at the *final* follow-up call will not actually turn up. For the first stage of recruitment (ie the initial call) the drop-out rate may be 50 per cent. This factor has to be considered when planning the recruitment and the resources needed for the work. It is this considerable fall-out rate together with the high cost of the venues which make clinics so very expensive.

Ideally, clinic respondents are recruited in such a way that they arrive at a steady rate throughout the day. This is difficult to achieve in practice, and lunchtime and early evening peaks must be expected and planned for.

Suitable incentives are needed when respondents are expected to give up time and travel to the venue. Unless the target respondents are very special, however, the incentive can be fairly modest. As for business-to-business respondents attending a group, a bottle of malt whisky is about adequate in the UK. If cash is more appropriate then a figure of twice the value of the whisky would have to be considered. Other encouragements to respondent attendance may include refreshments at the clinic. It is generally better to contract out this part of the work to a specialist caterer or use the facilities which the management of the venue can provide.

More important than either the incentive or refreshments is respondent interest in the subject of the clinic. At the initial recruitment stage the subject of the clinic must be 'sold'. Respondents are only likely to come if they anticipate an interesting event. However, there is an equal danger of 'overselling'. As in group discussion recruitment, a potential respondent may say 'yes' (and mean 'no') simply to get rid of a persistent recruiter.

RUNNING AND STAFFING THE CLINIC

Staffing levels depend on the number of respondents per day and how they are processed during the clinic. To get through 40 to 50 respondents a day requires around 8 to 12 staff at the clinic, excluding catering activities. Specific tasks of clinic staff include:

- **Reception.** Respondents should be welcomed as they arrive.
- **Pre-clinic interviewing.** Before seeing any products, interviews may be carried out to establish general behaviour patterns and perhaps perceptions prior to seeing products.
- **Clinic interviewing.** Respondents are interviewed as they look at products.
- **Post-clinic interviews.**
- **Checking** (and perhaps coding/processing) completed questionnaires.
- **General 'housekeeping' duties** — ensuring that the products are prepared for viewing, tidying up etc.

Individual staff can take it in turns to perform each of these tasks. Staffing requirements are unlikely to be the same throughout the day; recruitment work should provide a guide to the peaks and troughs of respondent traffic.

The use of self-completion questionnaires is often appropriate at a clinic. Respondents, for example, are given a clip board and questionnaire and complete rating scales as they examine the products. This approach reduces the interviewing staff levels required, as well as providing better quality responses since there is no possibility of 'interviewer bias'. Respondents, however, must be clearly instructed by clinic staff in how to use self-completion questionnaires.

In a clinic the hardest task is recruitment and, once there, the maximum contribution should be obtained from each respondent. It is therefore essential to ensure that self-completion questionnaires are checked *before* the respondents leave. More positively, it may be possible to carry out further depth research among respondent sub-groups after they complete the 'standard' clinic. Group discussions or individual de-briefings can, for example, be held.

As in a hall test, the activities of clinic staff must be organised and overseen by a supervisor. There must also be close liaison between the clinic and the base from which recruitment is carried out when the clinic spans several days. If attendance on the first day is poor, it may still be possible to compensate through a last-minute recruitment drive.

A clinic is frequently a substantial piece of research involving a large budget. Compared with other research work, the staff requirements are considerable. There is a major investment in recruitment work and the venue and associated facilities can involve major costs. The risks are therefore high. If respondents fail to attend in sufficient numbers the exercise will involve both wasted time and resources. More than in any other research, careful and detailed planning is essential for success.

DON'T FORGET THE BASICS

It is appropriate that this book finishes with a chapter on hall tests and clinics. These are amongst the most complicated of the market researcher's tasks in so far as they require meticulous planning, involve many people in their organisation and they are very expensive to administer. We researchers should take care to ensure that the excitement which can attach itself to complex and costly research techniques does not make us method-led, so we lose sight of the fundamentals of our work. After all, the hall test or the clinic is simply a venue for an interview to take place.

Whether interviewing takes place in a busy shopping precinct with clipboard in hand or on the telephone talking to a buyer in industry, the skills of drawing the truth out of people overshadow all other aspects of the research process. Hopefully, the reader who has persevered to this stage of the book will, by now, be convinced that good interviewing is at the heart of market research and, through the hints and wrinkles which have been discussed, will have honed their skills in finding out what is going on.

BIBLIOGRAPHY

∎

GENERAL READING ON MARKET RESEARCH (CONSUMER RESEARCH ORIENTATED)

Aaker, David A & George S Day (1990) *Marketing Research*, John Wiley, Chichester.

Baker, Michael J (1991) *Research for Marketing*, Macmillan, London.

Birn, R, Hague, P & Vangelder, P, (eds) (1990) *A Handbook of Market Research Techniques*, Kogan Page, London.

Birn, Robin (1991) *The Effective Use of Market Research*, Kogan Page, London.

Cannon, Tom (1973) *Advertising Research*, Intertext, Aylesbury.

Chisnall, Peter (1992) *Marketing Research*, McGraw-Hill, Maidenhead.

Chisnall, Peter (1991) *The Essence of Marketing Research*, Prentice Hall, Englewood Cliffs, New Jersey.

Crimp, Margaret (1990) *The Marketing Research Process*, Prentice-Hall, Englewood Cliffs, New Jersey.

Crouch, S (1984) *Marketing Research for Managers*, Heinemann, Oxford.

Ehrenberg, ASC (1988) *Repeat Buying*, Edward Arnold, Sevenoaks.

Gordon, Wendy & Roy Langmaid (1988) *Qualitative Market Research*, Gower, Aldershot.

Gorton, Keith & Isobel Doole (1989) *Low-Cost Marketing Research*, John Wiley & Sons, Chichester.

Green, P & Tull, J (1978) *Research for Marketing Decisions*, Prentice Hall, Englewood Cliffs, New Jersey.

Hague, Paul N & Peter Jackson (1990) *How To Do Marketing Research*, Kogan Page, London.

Hague, Paul N & Peter Jackson (1987) *Do Your Own Market Research*, Kogan Page, London.

Jain, AK, Pinson, P & Ratchford, B (1982) *Marketing Research — Applications and Problems*, John Wiley & Sons, Chichester.

Kreuger, Richard A (1989) *Focus Groups (A Practical Guide For Small Businesses)*, Sage Publications, London.

Robson, S & Foster, A (eds) (1989) *Qualitative Research in Action*, Edward Arnold, Sevenoaks.

Talmage, PA (1988) *Dictionary of Marketing Research*, Market Research Society, London.

Walker, R (ed) (1985) *Applied Qualitative Research*, Gower, Aldershot.

Williams, Keith (1981) *Behavioural Aspects of Marketing*, Heinemann, Oxford.

Worcester, RM & Downam, J (eds) (1986) *Consumer Market Research Handbook*, Elsevier, Netherlands.

GENERAL READING ON INDUSTRIAL MARKET RESEARCH

Hague, Paul N & Peter Jackson (1992) *Marketing Research in Practice*, Kogan Page, London.

MacLean, Ian (ed) (1976) *Handbook of Industrial Marketing Research*, Kluwer-Harrap, Brentford.

Stacey, N A H & Aubrey Wilson (1963) *Industrial Market Research — Management Techniques*, Hutchinson, London.

Sutherland, Ken (ed) (1991) *Researching Business Markets*, Kogan Page in association with the Industrial Marketing Research Association, London.

Wilson, Aubrey (1968) *The Assessment of Industrial Markets*, Hutchinson, London.

QUESTIONNAIRES

Hague, Paul (1993) *Questionnaire Design*, Kogan Page, London.

Oppenheim, AN (1970) *Questionnaire Design and Attitude Measurement*, Heinemann, Oxford.

Wolfe, A (1984) *Standardised Questions*, Market Research Society, London.

PRESENTATIONS AND REPORT WRITING

Jay, Anthony (1976) *Slide Rules*, Video Arts, London.

May, John (1982) *How To Make Effective Business Presentations*, McGraw-Hill, London.

JOURNALS AND PERIODICALS

Business Marketing Digest, (formerly *Industrial Marketing Digest*), quarterly, Wallington, Surrey.

Harvard Business Review, bi-monthly, Boston, Mass, US.

Journal of The Market Research Society, quarterly, London.

Marketing, weekly, London.

OTHER READING MATERIAL

Conference papers published each year by the Market Research Society and the Industrial Marketing Research Association.

INDEX

■